The lands of Rancho Pescadero, 1877
Map of San Mateo County; San Mateo County Historical Museum

Portraits of Pescadero

A memory album of five families and friends

BY TESS BLACK

A PESCADERO ORAL HISTORY

MUSIC BY PIANO AND BIRDS PRESS • LOMA MAR, CALIFORNIA

Portraits of Pescadero

A memory album of five families and friends

BY TESS BLACK

Published by

MUSIC BY PIANO & BIRDS PRESS

Loma Mar, California

Contact: P.O. Box 8, Pescadero, California 94060-0008   USA

Copyright © 2006 by Tess Black
All rights reserved.

ISBN: 0-9788514-0-4
Library of Congress Control Number: 2006907176

Editing, book design, layout, and pre-production by Ulu Tree in Loma Mar, California.
Printed by Community Printers, Inc. in Santa Cruz, California.

Cover photograph: View looking west of early Pescadero, mid-1850s to early 1860s.
From the Noel William Dias Collection in the Pescadero Historical Society archives.
Title page photographs: Mary Frances Plecarpo and Manuel Silveria Quadro;
Grace Shepherd Shaw; Harriet Helen Williamson and her brother, Earle Aaron ("Duke")
Williamson. All from collections in the Pescadero Historical Society archives.
Dedication page quote: Copyright © 2004 by Wendell Berry from Hannah Coulter.
Reprinted by permission of Shoemaker & Hoard.

"A lifetime's knowledge shimmers on the face of the land in the mind of a person who knows. The history of a place is the mind of an old man or an old woman who knows it, walking over it, and it is never fully handed on to anybody else, but has been mostly lost, generation after generation, going back and back to the first Indians."
— WENDELL BERRY

This book is dedicated with great affection to the people — past, present, and future — of the place called Pescadero.

Pescadero's main street—the San Gregorio or Old Stage Road—in 1913.

Introduction

Driving down Coast Highway from San Francisco, about 14 miles south of Half Moon Bay you crest a low hill and below you a view rises out of soft salt mists. On one side of the highway is the Pacific Ocean, advancing in long waves on rock stacks and sand dunes. On the other is the Pescadero Marsh, a wetland reserve of tule reeds and clumps of willow that is created by the union of two streams issuing several miles back in the Santa Cruz Mountains. Soon after crossing a bridge spanning the outlet of the marsh into the sea you see an "intersection" with a turn-lane accessing Pescadero Creek Road and a big sign planted in the field that reads, "Historic Pescadero, Est. 1856, 2 miles."

Pescadero Creek Road skirts the marsh, passes the fire station, and continues over a narrow bridge that in good weather barely clears the surface of Bútano Creek. Small houses begin to dot the roadside on the left, some of them simple wood frames adorned with embellishments popular in a long-ago era. On the right a broad, perfectly flat field of rich brown opens out, the descendant of an ancient riverbed, held in place by gently sculpted hills. An old creamery barn with "Level Lea Farm" stenciled in large letters on its roof stands across the road from Chandler Lane, a short spur leading off several yards past an attractive historic farm house and barn into the fields. At the four-way stop ahead a tall flagpole, a modest building which houses the post office, and a nineteenth-century church with its steeple missing signal the center of town.

According to the sign at the highway, this year marks the 150th anniversary of Pescadero town. Although Pescadero was never incorporated and has no official "date" to start its calendar, it was in 1856 that the first mercantile businesses started up near the Pescadero Creek ford. Public buildings were placed on a "town" grid of lots that had been drawn up by an enterprising San Francisco lawyer and a few other pioneering Americans in Santa Cruz who were moving into the area and buying up the old Mexican land grants. The 150-year history of Pescadero town is really their story. Theirs and the people who have ever lived here since—people who dug the earth; cut the trees; milked the cows; put up churches and stores, houses and schools; loved or grumbled about each other—and all the people who live here now.

In March of 2003 the Pescadero Oral History Project—a local group associated with The Pescadero Foundation, its nonprofit sponsor—launched a series of recorded interviews with longtime Pescadero residents spearheaded by myself and a fellow Project member, Sande Low. Our intention was to preserve and pass along some of these early town stories as told by Pescadero people. We were initially funded by a grant from the Peninsula Community Foundation in San Mateo County but continued on with our work long after the funding was gone, collecting hours of video- and audiotape, scanning photographs and documents from private family albums, and researching in county historical institutions. This book is the result.

Portraits of Pescadero is not meant to be a "scholarly" history. It's an intimate family story told in roughly sequential segments, pieced together from the oral histories, genealogies, and photographic images archived so far, and from personal accounts found in books and records already published. Although I've tried to be as accurate as possible, there are bound to be errors in the text. The public records in themselves often present incomplete or conflicting data, or information that is sometimes skewed by the prevailing attitudes of past times and limited by the "known facts" available to the people who wrote them. The nature of human memory is such that in every moment of time the ultimate "truth" about anything can only be measured against a given point of view that is itself based on *personal* experience and *personal* knowledge. There is always more to be discovered, learned, or recovered, as each generation adds its own perspective. I expect that what we now know about the history of Pescadero will continue to be clarified and reshaped.

There are also many stories missing of people who have greatly contributed to the town's life and character—those of the Mexican; Portuguese; Italian; Chinese; Japanese; and Filipino peoples, in particular—some of whom have lived here in large numbers at different times over the past 150 years. Among them are the stories about individuals and families—such as the Duarte family that started doing business in Pescadero in 1894—who are vital members of today's community. Although I originally thought 150 years was a relatively short span of time to cover, I soon realized that if I were to be thorough in the telling of a single family story, following the thread back from the living person speaking to me today to her ancestors who first arrived in California in the 1850s, I would be faced with a task requiring months of effort. Multiplied by even so small a number as the 30 people interviewed, my first intentions had to be scaled down.

I decided to focus on the five families that originally settled the township in its first 20 years and that have descendants still residing here. They are the Moores; Weeks; Shaws; McCormicks; and Steeles. Each chapter begins with an introduction to the contemporary family member with whom we conducted interviews, then jumps back in time to the founding pioneer generation. I try to answer the following questions: Who were they? Where did they come from? What was the world (the nation, their town, their family) like then? Why did they emigrate to this isolated Coastal region and how did they manage to get here? What were the memorable events and relationships in their lives? Why did some stay, and others leave?

As each story moves forward again to the present, I let the words of these fourth- and even fifth-generation Pescaderans give the answers whenever possible: Clifford James Moore; Frances Bell Weeks (Dubel); Elaine Baldwin Shaw (Steele); Sister Marie Elise McCormick; and Ruth Louise Steele (Moore). Other remembrances, taken from our interviews with neighbors and friends, and interviews recorded previously by other historians, join in to create a dynamic picture of Pescadero's early days and how the town grew.

Genealogies and photographs give added depth to these "windows" into the past. Each of the families has a cast of characters that is listed as a simplified family tree at the beginning of the story. I focus primarily on the names of people who appear in the text (most often highlighted in bold face), and do not always list their descendants or follow other offshoots of the family. Shaded names indicate the lineage from pioneer ancestors to present-generation Pescaderans. Each chapter also has an installment of an abbreviated timeline to give a broader context for what was happening in the town. This running timeline shows how remarkably the family stories parallel many of the historical, political, and social events occurring in the world, the nation, and the state—the great Western Migration; the Gold Rush; California statehood; technological advances; and several wars and depressions, for example.

These are stories about an "ordinary" American place, told by "ordinary" people who were sometimes called upon to do extraordinary things just to stay alive, let alone prosper. We meet men of energy and ambition, and women of enormous resourcefulness and secret courage. We hear tales of adversity and endurance, but also of satisfying accomplishment and simple, abiding pleasures. Good or bad, every facet of human personality has its moment on this small stage, but most of the memories you will read here reflect most strongly the quiet beauty of many old-fashioned community values: peacefulness; honest work; friendship; cooperation in hard times; the love and strength nurtured by family. I hope that these virtues will constitute Pescadero's legacy to its people and to you for a long, long time to come.

Tess Black, Loma Mar, September 2006

Acknowledgements

There are many people without whose knowledge, hard work, and good will this book would never have been. Some of them are friends and relatives of the families who have been interested in their own genealogies; others are those who, either by profession or avocation, have devoted their passionate energy to researching Coast history in general and all things relating to the Pescadero area in particular. They have given me direction in many panicky hours when I thought the puzzle with its interlocking pieces was too big to put together or the truth impossible to tell. I am grateful to all, but am especially indebted to the following people for their contributions:

Thanks to Sandra Norris-Low, a woman of great and heartful aspiration, for the wonderful work we did together giving birth to "Voices of Pescadero," and for getting me launched;

Thanks to Frances Dubel, our first interviewee, for her intelligence, openness, her gloriously spunky nature, and for giving us an introduction to her circle of friends;

Thanks to her brother, Edward Weeks, faithful custodian of the town's ever-changing enrollment, a humble man whose goodness of heart and strength of character never fail;

Thanks to Kiyo Matsuki (Elizabeth Morimoto), for inspiration, delightful company, her gift for storytelling, and for her widely embracing appreciation of all that life may bring to us;

Thanks to Elaine Steele, a real lady, for her generosity of spirit, her willingness to share her family secrets and photographs, and her enduring grace and humor;

Thanks to Clifford Moore, salt of the earth, a man you can trust for his steadfastness and honesty, a true Native Son and a true friend;

Gratitude forever to Ruth Moore, for everything—for countless opened doors, for good fun, making me feel at home, and for the great gift of her friendship;

Thanks to Bob DeLapp for supporting me in every possible way for the past three years, for showing me the wisdom of standing still in one place, and for his most amazing love.

McCORMICK FAMILY STORY
Sister Marie Elise McCormick
Joan McCormick and Karen Nyeland
Mary Pat Dougherty Kanzaki
Marty McCormick
Delight **Durant** Castle
Lisa Tune and Kate Meyers

MOORE FAMILY STORY
Clifford James Moore
Ruth **Steele** Moore
David Brock and Christophe Lecuyer, *The Chemical Heritage Foundation*

SHAW FAMILY STORY
Elaine **Shaw** Steele
John Elias Shaw Jr.
Lois **Vierra** Offill

STEELE FAMILY STORY
Elaine **Shaw** Steele
Ruth Louise **Steele** Moore
Betsy Bradley, *Coastways Ranch*
Dorothy **Atkins** Hudson and Anne **Atkins** Robinson, *Coastways Ranch*
Jon and Cate Hudson, *Coastways Ranch*
Tim Hudson, *Coastways Ranch*

WEEKS FAMILY STORY
Edward and Marie Weeks
Frances **Weeks** Dubel
Ruth **Dubel** Ditty
Meredith Reynolds
Pam McReynolds
Walter and Aida Hohl
Norma Hohl

HISTORIANS
Clinton Blount,
Albion Environmental, Inc.
Gina Capers,
*Vice President and Archivist of the
Spanishtown Historical Society*
Velia Garcia,
Department Chair of Anthropology at SFSU
Mark Hylkema,
California State Parks archaeologist
Sandy Lydon,
Historian Emeritus, Cabrillo College
Carol Peterson,
San Mateo County Historical Museum
Mike Svanevic,
California State Parks historian

Peas are as popular a staple grown by farmers in Pescadero today as they were 150 years ago.

Early vegetable crate label courtesy of Kay Nelson.

ORAL HISTORY PROJECT
Lynne Bowman
Patricia Carr
Meg Delano
John Dixon
Sande Low
Janet Murphy
Maeva and John Neale
Kay Nelson
Cotton and Rob Skinner
Greg and Ann Timm

PESCADERO PEOPLE
David Augustine,
California State Parks ranger
Norm Benedetti
Debbie Bennett
Irv and Jesse Blomquist
Socorro Brown
Geraldine **Quadro** Burns
The Community Church Ladies' Guild
The Great Noel Dias,
and his niece, Peggy White
Ron Duarte
Kathy Duarte
Susan Friedman
Janet Jarvis
Elizabeth **Morimoto** Matsuki
Rita **Cabuag** Prigan
Debbie Vento

AT LARGE
Robert Buelteman,
Peninsula Community Foundation
Clifford Pierce
Faust Silvestri and his daughter,
Laura Silvestri

Contents

13 — *The Moore Family* / Clifford James Moore
   14 — *The Pioneer Generation*
      15 — *Family Tree*
      22 — *Timeline: 1822 – 1856*
   29 — *Rancho Pescadero 1833 – 1852 and beyond*
   39 — *Ever Since 1853*

47 — *The Weeks Family* / Frances Bell Weeks
   48 — *The Pioneer Generation*
      49 — *Family Tree*
      54 — *Timeline 1856 – 1879*
   58 — *The House on Goulson Street*

73 — *The Shaw Family* / Elaine Baldwin Shaw
   74 — *The Pioneer Generation*
      75 — *Family Tree*
   81 — *Pescadero – 1866 to 1900s*
      88 — *Sidebar: The Diary of Bertha Shaw, 1883 – 1884*
      92 — *Timeline 1880 – 1900*
      96 — *Sidebar: Frank George*

105 — *The McCormick Family* / Sister Marie Elise McCormick
   106 — *The Pioneer Generation*
      107 — *Family Tree*
      112 — *Timeline 1900 – 1930*
   123 — *The Roaring Twenties*

131 — *The Steele Family* / Ruth Louise Steele
   132 — *The Pioneer Generation*
      133 — *Family Tree*
      138 — *Timeline 1930 – 1950*
   142 — *A Dairy Empire*
   150 — *A 100-Year Legacy*

The Moore Family
Clifford James Moore

Clifford Moore holds the rifle his great-grandfather, Alexander Moore, brought across the Plains in 1847. September 2, 2004.

*I*n a green field near his house on North Street, a wooden sign reads: "Moore Ranch, Ever Since 1853." Clifford Moore, a true Native Son, is one of the last of the old-time families who have held tenure in this place for more than 150 years. His ancestors, great-grandparents Alexander and Adaline Moore, moved here in 1853. At that time there was little more than an adobe dwelling and a few people needed to tend the old Spanish land grant and its scattered herds of cattle, a portion of which Alex's father, Eli Moore, had just bought. The Moores were the first to build a beautiful frame house near a curve in the creek, and in a few short years establish the town of Pescadero with some other energetic Yankee pioneers. Clifford lives on the last 100 acres in Pescadero that are still held in the Moore name. His wife of fifty years, the former Ruth Louise Steele, is also a fourth-generation Pescaderan, raised in the dairy farm country at Año Nuevo.

Retired from public work, Cliff is still a man of the land and still keeps his hand in, repairing machinery, grooming the fields, and hauling feed. On any given day as you drive by his place just northeast of town you might see 73-year-old Cliff, wearing a hat to keep off the sun, driving his tractor, cutting hay, weed-whacking the grass by the side of the road, or helping his son, Jim, a master carpenter, as he puts on a new roof for the old dairy barn. Thirty head of fat Red Angus cattle dot the green and yellow hillsides in back. Cliff keeps the cows because he's known cattle all his life; they don't earn him a living, but they help pay the taxes. He might say, if you take care of the land, it takes care of you. That is work that can carry you for a lifetime.

The Pioneer Generation

"In essentials, unity; in nonessentials, liberty; and in all things, love."

— Motto of the Moravian Church

Wedding portraits of Pescadero pioneers Adaline Rebecca Spainhower, 24, and Alexander Moore, 20, taken in 1847.

FREEDOM, PERSEVERANCE, AND THE "LOVE FEAST"

Adaline Rebecca Spainhower came into the world on July 28, 1822 in Stokes County, North Carolina, one of 13 children born to Daniel Spainhower and Mary Magdalene Hauser. The Spainhowers were members of a Swiss Moravian community centered at Winston-Salem, North Carolina, the second of two such provinces in America founded by the Moravian Church.

Originating in what is now the Czech Republic in the fifteenth century, the Moravians were some of the earliest Protestants. Sixty years before Martin Luther began his reformation, the newly founded church looked for a return to the pure practices of early Christianity and the "love feast." In the following centuries the Moravians were hounded from place to place for their religious beliefs and eventually journeyed to the New World.

The American story of the Spainhower family begins in 1740 when Adaline's ancestor, Johann Heinrich Spainhauer, emigrated from Central Europe. He found asylum in a fledgling Moravian settlement in Pennsylvania, then, in a few years' time, relocated to a second colony established in the Piedmont section of North Carolina where other groups seeking religious freedom—such as the Quakers—had also settled. Adaline's family lived near Bethania.

Adaline grew up as part of a large, expansive family in an atmosphere of cooperation, love, and respect for others; from her girlhood she witnessed and probably assisted at the births of many of her younger siblings. These early experiences were to serve her well when she became an adult.

The moral character defined by Adaline's family and girlhood community was at odds with the rest of North Carolina. At the time she was born, out of a population of nearly 650,000 people

The Moore Family

I. ELI MOORE [b. 1805 North Carolina – 6/6/1859 Santa Cruz] *m.* **LIZBETH "SADDIE" PALMER** [4/12/1806 North Carolina – 1859 Santa Cruz].

    II. ALEXANDER MOORE (12/17/1826 Tennessee – 8/26/1902 Pescadero) on 2/2/1847 *m.* **ADALINE REBECCA SPAINHOWER** (7/28/1822 North Carolina – 1/24/1902 Pescadero)

        III. Eli Daniel Moore (12/12/1847 Santa Cruz – ?] *m.* Ellen McCormick

        III. Joseph Ladd Moore (3/27/1849 Santa Cruz – ?) on 12/25/1877 *m.* Emma Thompson (6/14/1889 Vermont – 7/19/1904 Pescadero). Seven children.

        III. Mary Rebecca Moore (9/7/1850 Santa Cruz – 9/17/1850 Santa Cruz)

        III. WILLIAM ALEXANDER MOORE (7/19/1851 Santa Cruz – April 1936) *m.* **HATTIE HUFF** (5/14/1856 Maine – 7/26/1940 Pescadero)

            IV. JAMES ALEXANDER MOORE (12/12/1888 – 4/8/1958) *m.* **ANNIE CABRAL** (b. 9/20/1905)

                V. CLIFFORD JAMES MOORE (5/15/1933) *m.* **RUTH LOUISE STEELE** (4/8/1938)

        III. George T. Moore (3/5/1853 Santa Cruz – 3/1/1865 Pescadero)

        III. John Eli Moore (5/20/1854 Santa Cruz – 4/1/1865 Pescadero)

        III. Ida Jane Moore (5/28/1856 Pescadero – 10/30/1947) on 3/15/1879 *m.* **Charles Edward Steele Sr.** (3/6/1851 Amherst, Ohio – 12/9/1930 California). Children: Mae Chloe Steele; Norman Steele Sr.; Grover Steele; Charlie Steele Jr.; Perle Ella Steele.

        III. David Eugene Moore (3/26/1858 Pescadero – 10/29/1927) on 2/24/1884 *m.* Mary S. Hayward (8/12/1863 San Francisco – ?)

        III. Walter Henry Moore (6/14/1864 Pescadero – 12/9/1909 Pescadero) *m.* **Frances H. Cuff** (Palmer) (1/16/1865 San Francisco – 3/21/1937)

            IV. Ida Moore *m.* Joseph Mesquite

            IV. Louise Alice Moore (6/18/1892 Pescadero – 1975) in 1909 *m.* **Frank Grant Williamson** (7/04/1885 – 12/10/1963). Earle Aaron ("Duke") Williamson and Harriet Helen Williamson.

            IV. Walter Harold Moore (3/28/1893 Pescadero – 8/24/1977) on 11/11/1924 *m.* **Florence Almira Williamson** (10/02/1894 Pescadero – 9/24/1972). Walter Ellsworth Moore III; Gordon Earle Moore; Francis Allen Moore.

    II. Thomas Walker Moore (6/20/1832 – 9/13/1914)

    II. Rachel, William, Emeline, and **Elizabeth Moore**

roughly a third were slaves. Against this background, the Spainhower family supported the cause of freedom and their belief in simple goodness. All of the Spainhower children were probably well schooled, as the Moravians' attitude toward education was remarkably progressive. The Salem Female Academy founded by the Moravian Church—one of the earliest institutions in the country devoted to the education of women—had already been up and running for 20 years when Adaline was born.

Adaline was 18 when she embarked on the first great journey of her life. On April 23, 1840 her family, headed by her 58-year-old father, left Winston-Salem in a covered wagon train bound for Missouri. They traveled in company with her first cousin, Elijah Spainhower; his wife and children; Elijah's mother, Elizabeth; and his blind sister, Rebecca. It took nine weeks for the company to cover a distance of 1,115 miles.

Adaline's family settled near Elijah's in what is now Johnson County, in the west-central portion of Missouri. And Johnson County abutted the county of Jackson, where Adaline was soon to meet her future destiny in the person of young Alexander Moore.

The Jumping-Off Place

We don't know for sure whether or not the Moore and the Spainhower families were acquainted before they met in Missouri, or—if they were previously connected in the North Carolina days—how closely. But Ruth Moore, reflecting recently on the results of genealogical research she did some years ago, thinks the two families might have been linked as far back as eighteenth-century Europe. In any case, a close bond between the two families was very likely strengthened by their proximity during the Missouri years.

Alexander was born in Tennessee on December 17, 1826 to Eli and Lizbeth "Saddie" Palmer Moore. Eli Moore was a farmer. Although no specific records have yet been found to indicate he ever owned land prior to moving West, judging by his subsequent success in California he was a man of great energy and inner resources.

At age 30, Eli grew restless in the depression of the 1830s. Just across the Mississippi River in neighboring Missouri, a great ruckus was going on, and Eli thought he saw better prospects for a himself there. In 1835 he and his wife gathered their family—their oldest son, 9-year-old Alexander; daughter Rachel; and two younger boys, Thomas and William—and moved to Jackson County, poised on the edge of the western frontier.

Jackson County was home to the rapidly growing trade center of Independence. After the territory had been acquired as part of the Louisiana Purchase in 1803 and later admitted as a "slave" state in The Missouri Compromise of 1821, land-hungry Americans "discovered" how fine it was and began to pour in. Independence—the Jackson County seat—was happening. Located only three miles north of the Missouri River, a major transportation artery, it was an ideal outfitting center, servicing Yankee and Mexican merchants who traversed the Santa Fe Trail and pioneers braving the new Oregon Trail.

Eli Moore made good use of his time in Missouri. By the mid-1840s his own family was growing with two more daughters, Emeline and Elizebeth. His oldest son, Alexander, was nearly of age and looking to marry, and the younger boys, too, were coming along quick. Eli watched the surrounding country bulge at the seams from the overspill of the cities on the eastern seaboard. Missouri was getting too crowded, what with people all fired up by the notion of "Manifest Destiny." There was no stopping them, folks kept pushing west in search of more room, setting up in one remote area after another only to have to move on again when that country got too thick with people.

The whole country was talking about the journals and diaries brought back by the Lewis and

Portrait of a dream: Pescadero town as it appeared around the turn of the last century.

Clark Expedition; the books, the newspaper and magazine articles written by such men as Richard Henry Dana and John Charles Frémont; and tales told around family hearths by returning frontiersmen. In 1843 the "Great Migration" really kicked off as hundreds and then thousands converged on Independence, enriched the local merchants in the process of getting themselves outfitted, and set their course West in rising clouds of dust and hope.

As the excitement grew all around them, Eli Moore and his neighbors and friends started planning to embark in search of new land themselves. Such an undertaking required a lot of money and a lot of goods. Some folks had to prepare for years to gather together everything they might need for the journey and for resettlement. In the last months before their departure, the Spainhower and Moore families merged their resources and irrevocably forged their alliance when on February 2, 1847 Adaline Rebecca Spainhower, age 24, married Alexander Moore, 20, in Adaline's home county of Johnson.

COFFEE AND BACON

On May 9, 1847 the Moores—Eli's family, and Alexander and Adaline—hitched up an ox team and left Independence with about 200 other souls bound for Oregon and—maybe—California. In the three short months following Alexander and Adaline's wedding, the Moores worked feverishly to finish gathering household furnishings, farm equipment, food, clothing, livestock, and cash to take with them. They said goodbye to friends and loved ones they probably expected never to see again in this life.

When the wagon train left Missouri the Mexican/American War, fueled by the American government's dreams of expansion, had been rum-

The Moore Family 17

bling throughout the Southwest for over a year, but its outcome was still uncertain. This was reason enough for most folks to favor the route to Oregon, but some were still undecided. After traveling 1,200 miles the emigrants reached the Big Sandy River at a point west of the Fort Hall trading post. There they met up with Brigadier General Stephen Watts Kearny and Lieutenant Colonel John Charles Frémont as they were headed east to Leavenworth. What they had to say changed several minds within a few hours' time.

The two officers maintained separate camps. According to William Trubody, one of the Moores' fellow travelers, Kearny was "offish and high-hat," a man apparently so impressed with his own importance that he couldn't be bothered to come over to the emigrants' camp—they would have to come to him. Kearny's main point was to discourage anyone from crossing the snowbound Sierras into California and to keep on for Oregon. The terrible events that had befallen the Donner Party earlier in the year were still vivid in everyone's minds and Kearny's warnings seemed sensible.

Frémont's character was very different. Positive and personable, he visited the emigrants' camp readily and made a most profound impression on the Moore men. The famous "Pathfinder" was a veteran of three exploratory expeditions to the Pacific Coast made over the previous five years. Eli must have been familiar with Frémont's widely-read account of these adventures and recognized a kindred soul in the man. Frémont assured the emigrants that the war with Mexico was indeed over and although the Treaty of Guadalupe Hidalgo was not yet ratified California was open to American settlement. Whatever they were looking for—farm, pasture, or timberland—they could take their pick. And as to any lingering doubts raised by the Donner Party disaster, Frémont advised them to avoid delays, keep moving along, and be sure to cross the mountains before the winter storms set in.

The wagons left Fort Hall and went down the Snake River to the spot where the roads divided between Oregon and California. A decision had to be made for those who were still weighing the odds. The Moores decided on California. Everyone who had come this far together had grown very close from months of shared experience, much of it unimaginably hard. This parting of the ways was a second kind of death, akin to their departure from Independence, and farewells were deeply emotional as the travelers split off.

"So they hashed it out; the Moores and the Coopers and two others broke off of that train, and came over Donner Pass—the first [people] to come over Donner after the Donner Party had perished." — Clifford Moore, 2003

The Moores branched off to California with about 15 other families: 50 men and 50 women and children; 20 wagons and 120 oxen. They elected Captain Charley Hopper as their guide. A seasoned frontiersman, trapper, and hunter, in '41 he'd accompanied the Bidwell-Bartleson party with the first wagon train of emigrants to split off from the Oregon Trail and cross the Sierras into Mexican California. He knew the territory well and was an excellent provider. When the emigrants were tired of having nothing more to eat than coffee and bacon for days on end, Hopper would disappear for a few hours and return with enough antelope meat to satisfy them all.

The party crossed the Goose Creek Mountains and then went down the Humboldt River. William Trubody remarks that the next 40 miles of sand and sagebrush were the most trying of the whole journey. They crossed it at night to avoid the burning heat of day and to conserve water. Finally they made it to the Truckee River and followed it, laboriously crossing and re-crossing it many times as they went.

The Moores and the others over-nighted at the Donner Camp on the approach to the Sierras and burned everything they could spare to lighten their load before crossing the summit. On the other side they soon struck the Bear River and continued on to reach Johnson's Ranch on October 2, 1847.

A MILE SQUARE

In an effort to attract settlers who would put down roots and make a real investment in the place, the existing government had offered to give 11 leagues of land to anyone who would settle permanently at Stockton. Hearing of the emigrants' arrival, a Captain Weber rode off to acquaint the new arrivals with this proposal.

When Eli and Alexander Moore's families crossed the Plains from Missouri to California, with their Yankee inventions and farm equipment in tow, they did not have a thresher. Below, Alexander Moore proudly exhibits the first "modern" thresher in Pescadero town. Ca. 1900.

He met them at Sutter's Fort and offered Alexander Moore a tract of land that was "a mile square," [640 acres] and two city lots if he would stay at Stockton. One man had already taken him up on his proposal but was "cleaned out by the Indians and small pox" the year before. Undaunted, Alexander thought this a fine idea.

He could hardly believe his luck—not yet 21, and within just a few days of arriving in California he'd already been offered the chance to become a land and house owner! The October weather was still fine, but the days were already getting shorter and November was not far off. Adaline was very pregnant with the child they'd conceived most likely on their wedding night eight months past and she would need a comfortable shelter and some women around her soon. Along with Charley Hopper and five or six of the others in their group Alexander accepted Weber's offer.

Lizbeth Moore, Alexander Moore's mother, in Santa Cruz. 1850s.

The Moore Family 19

Above: *On a hunting party, Alexander Moore is seated on his horse, Rattler. At his right is Dr. Murphy, of San Francisco, and on his left, William McCormick. The ghostly shadows in the foreground are hunting dogs.*

Below: *"The Moore Boys"—From left to right: Bill Moore; the first Walter Moore; David Moore; Joe Moore; Charles Steele Sr. (Ida Jane Moore's husband). Early 1890s.*

But his father, Eli, wanted to keep moving. He remembered what he'd heard around that campfire on the Big Sandy, listening to Frémont's glowing accounts of the country around Santa Cruz. He trusted that the man knew what he was talking about. If Frémont said that that area was "the most beautiful place in California," that was where Eli wanted to go.

Alexander left his wife and their effects on the ground at Stockton in the care of the others who had chosen to stay and went with his father's family and the rest of their party to help them cross the San Joaquin River. When they got there Eli took a stand, refusing to go on without his son and his daughter-in-law. He took 10 mules and went back to fetch Adaline. His arguments were so convincing that when he showed up again at the San Joaquin he not only had Adaline in tow but all the others who had decided to invest in Stockton too!

Alexander's memoir tells the story of what happened next. The San Joaquin had neither a bridge nor a ferry, but the men were resourceful. They made a 16-x-16-foot raft by tying willow poles together, then stuffed the spaces between with tule rushes and placed a woven mat of tules on top to make a floor. A few of the men swam across the current carrying a towing rope attached to the raft. When the raft was pulled across, the wagon was offloaded and the empty raft towed back to be reloaded with another wagon. It took a whole day to get the party across. As it grew dark on that crisp October evening, young Alexander earned his first $3 in California, paid to him by two men he helped cross the river in this way.

The Moores and their friends continued on to Mission San Jose and camped on the old Santa Clara Road. Once again the party divided up, some going to Monterey—the former capital of Alta California—and the rest to Santa Cruz. The Moores veered south, pressing on towards the mountains, and set up cabins near where the Lexington Reservoir is now with the idea of wintering there.

Eli and Alexander laid plans to erect a mill for Ike Brennan [Isaac Branham]. But in early November Alexander went on a little jaunt to Santa Cruz accompanied by an acquaintance named Mr. Doke to see what it was like. Along the way they met two vivid Santa Cruz characters, one of whom was Captain Isaac Graham. Alexander liked Graham's raw, robust spirit and he liked everything he saw in the adobe pueblo of Santa Cruz. In fact, he was so enthusiastic that when he returned to camp he told his friends and family that he liked it and the people there better than any part of California he had yet seen.

His father and Charley Hopper, escorted again by Mr. Doke, promptly rode off to see for themselves. Eli was bowled over. Not a man to waste time once he'd made up his mind, he bought a ranch practically on the spot from Don José Antonio Bolcoff, who was then Justice of the Peace at Santa Cruz. It was the first land ever directly conveyed to an American in that part of the country.

Back at the camp, Eli's will overcame all argument. The family abandoned thoughts of hanging on through the winter in their little cabin and packed up their gear. The only road that could accommodate their heavy wagons took them back by way of San Jose, Gilroy, and Pajaro.

One night they camped under a large sycamore tree near present-day Watsonville. Before they left the next day an enormous wolf dashed right inside the wagon circle and seized one of their sheep. Alexander was hopping mad. He had gone to too much trouble "fetching" their precious livestock all the way across the Plains, keeping them alive and healthy, only to have them stolen at the journey's end by wild predators.

The local people told him that this particular wolf was "a terror to the nature all around them." Several attempts had already been made to catch and kill it, but all had failed. Alexander determined to avenge his loss and win glory for himself by bagging the legendary beast.

"We took the dead sheep and placed it on a little rising ground. Capt. Hopper and myself took our places on the slope behind it, armed with double-barreled shotguns loaded with buckshot. Each [of us] wrapped in a buffalo robe, we patiently waited for Mr. Wolf. Hopper, being an old, lucky mountain hunter, had learned to imitate the cry of a wolf. When everything was quiet he gave the cry. It was soon answered.

"The first time the wolf was too quick for us. He seized the dead sheep and before either of us could get a shot at him, was running off with it, but we succeeded in making him drop it. When he made his appearance again a short time after, a shot from my gun laid him out.

"He proved to be an unusually large black wolf. His hide was nearly as large as a bullock's. As soon as it was known that we had killed the wolf, the Spaniards and residents came flocking into the camp to see the hide and rejoice at his death."

— *Alexander Moore, A pioneer of '47*

The Moores reached Santa Cruz on November 15, 1847 and camped the first night on the plaza by the mission church. Then they moved into an old adobe building that belonged to Don José Bolcoff, the man from whom Eli had purchased his land. Adaline, exhausted from months of enduring dirt, poor food, sickness, and hard physical labor, was in the final month of her pregnancy. Winter was upon them and they were all glad to rest. Sometime during the following month the Alcalde (Governor) William Blackburn gave Eli Moore another piece of land on a portion of which

Timeline 1822 – 1856
Highlighted parallel events in San Francisco Bay Area, California, and the Nation

1776 Mission Dolores—or San Francisco de Asís—founded by Moraga at Yerba Buena.

1822 Mexico wins its freedom from Spain.

1830s The great age of railroad proliferation begins and continues through the 1860s. Frontiersmen begin to penetrate into the Mexican country of Alta California.

Frenchman Louis Daguerre captures images on film using metal plates—the beginning of popular photography for the masses.

1833 The Mexican government of Alta California starts dividing up land and granting huge allotments to Mexican citizens.

1834 The Franciscan missions are disestablished in Alta California.

1836 The Revolution of 1836, led by Alvarez and Castro, takes place against the Mexico City authorities.

1837 The great 64-year Victorian Age begins as Queen Victoria ascends Britain's throne.

1841 The Bidwell–Bartleson Party is the first emigrant wagon train to reach California from Missouri.

1845 James K. Polk, a Democrat and a major proponent of Manifest Destiny, is inaugurated as President.

1846 On May 11, the Mexican-American War begins in Texas. On June 6, The Bear Flag Republic initiates American take-over of California.

Out of an estimated aboriginal population of 250,000 there are now 98,000 Native Californians.

1847 On January 30, Yerba Buena is officially renamed San Francisco.

1848 James Marshall discovers gold at Sutter's Mill on January 24.

On February 2, the Treaty of Guadalupe Hidalgo officially ends the Mexican-American War and California territory is accessed by the United States. The population in California is about 18,000.

1849 The Gold Rush begins and in the great land rush that ensues large-scale agriculture and dairying enterprises grow rapidly as the Yankees take over.

Zachary Taylor is inaugurated as president but dies after a year in office; Vice President Millard Fillmore takes over.

California Lodge No.1 of the International Order of Oddfellows is established in San Francisco.

the courthouse of Santa Cruz stands today. Eli put up the first frame dwelling to be built in that area and moved into it with his wife and family in January. Alexander and Adaline would have to wait until spring to build their own house.

Santa Cruz – 1847

The town at Santa Cruz was only nine years older than 47-year-old Eli at the time the Moores came. Since its founding by the Spanish as a Franciscan mission in 1791, Santa Cruz had grown from a small frontier outpost, remotely associated with the presidio at Yerba Buena [San Francisco] and more closely with the one at Monterey, into a community of over 600 people.

Alta California had become a Mexican province in 1822 when Mexico threw off Spanish rule. The officials in Mexico City appointed a governor to head the provincial legislature that met in the region's capital at the Monterey presidio and the colorful Californio Era began, blooming like a desert wildflower for a brief quarter century.

It was a time of both gracious living and turbulent politics. The five-year period from 1831 to 1836 was particularly chaotic. Eleven different governors came and went and with each change of administration, the Californios, especially from the Santa Cruz area north, grew increasingly disgruntled. Mexico City was too far away—it might as well be in Spain! The northern Californios wanted more influence over the political authorities in Monterey, if not absolute self-rule.

Logging begins in San Mateo County with the first power-driven sawmill at Woodside.

Whaling also begins on the Coast as hundreds of Azorean Portuguese begin to immigrate into California.

1850 California joins the Union as the 31st state on September 9.

Four great fires occur in San Francisco costing millions of dollars.

1851 Two more great fires occur in San Francisco, whose population is now estimated at 30,000. The Vigilantes start up. By the end of the year 25,000 Chinese are living in California; this number increases to 47,000 by 1860.

1856 San Mateo County is formed as a separate entity from San Francisco and confirmed on April 18, 1857. (Pescadero is still in Santa Cruz County and does not become part of San Mateo until 1868.)

Early American adventurers, seeking their fortunes in a variety of ways, began exploring Alta California in the 1830s. This book cover from Grace Shaw's Memory Album gives a nice suggestion of these rough-hewn characters.

In 1836 Juan Bautista Alvarado, then the senior member of the territorial legislature in Monterey, led a rebellious assault against the presidio and forced the governor to surrender. The coup was staged with the help of Alvarado's longtime friend, José Castro, and the political support of Mariano Vallejo. It was also backed by a rowdy contingent of foreigners led by Isaac Graham, an American then residing in the Pajaro Valley.

Graham wanted complete independence from the Mexican government—in fact, he was vehemently opposed to having any kind of association with it; Alvarado favored remaining part of Mexico but with greater local autonomy. The Mexican authorities saw Alvarado as a moderate and after the revolt appointed him governor and Castro, president of the legislature. The two formed a militia with themselves as colonels.

The rancheros imported three kinds of cattle to run on their land grants: the Gallego of Northern Spain, which was a light yellowish fawn color; the Castilian of Central Spain, dusky or near black; and the Andalusian of Southern Spain, which had variations in color. They also brought a long-haired sheep called the churro from Spain.

Their game still wasn't won. The council in Los Angeles stayed loyal to Mexico and refused to recognize Alvarado's authority. Tensions between the northern and southern factions of Alta California persisted over the next several years, sometimes erupting in fights that included government troops.

Courtesy David Augustine, California State Parks

Alvarado triumphed long enough to maintain a stable government for about four years. Then various new attempts at revolt broke out in the early 1840s. Isaac Graham led many of these actions, but he was not to see the realization of his dream of California's independence until the Bear Flag Republic of 1847.

Meanwhile, beginning in 1831 the government of Alta California tried to follow through with the original Spanish plan to secularize the missions at some future point by replacing the padres with a lay clergy, dispersing lands among the aboriginal people who'd provided the bulk of the labor force under the padres' direction, and converting the mission centers into pueblos [towns] or presidios. With the demise of the Franciscan priests' influence and a scattered population composed mostly of former Spanish and Mexican soldiers, what actually happened is that the lands were divided into enormous chunks and granted to individuals who'd served in the military or who were friends of the current administrators. These lucky families owned thousands of acres of cattle range and grew fabulously wealthy selling hides and tallow.

When the Moores arrived in Santa Cruz the mission at Villa de Branciforte had been converted into a presidio and administrative center; the pueblo served as the county seat.

The Mexican town had a lot to offer. Conveniently located on a coastline that offered very few viable harbors, it was a main shipping point for a number of burgeoning industries in the surrounding country: hides and tallow off the vast cattle ranches; whale oil; sea otter and beaver pelts; farm and orchard crops. Ships of many nations brought in merchandise from Asia and the Pacific, from South America, and from New York. The sandstone hills around Santa Cruz, commonly called "chalk rock," also supported limestone quarrying as one of the town's earliest industries. Native forests of gigantic redwoods made the lumber industry extremely profitable too. Timber prices would soar during the 1850s and early 1860s after the Gold Rush set off a mushrooming construction boom in San Francisco.

All this activity created a community that grew incrementally more and more "cosmopolitan." During the 1820s and '30s the first Americans and other foreigners trickled into Branciforte. They were mountaineers, adventurers, hunters, and trappers, men seeking their fortunes in the lucrative fur trade. The Mexican government let them alone for the most part, which suited everyone, but if a foreigner agreed to convert to the Catholic faith and could guarantee he would earn an income of at least a $1,000 a year, he was eligible to become a Mexican citizen with the right to own property. A few took advantage of this offer and joined the ranks of wealthy ranch owners. Some assimilated even more completely by marrying into prominent Mexican families.

By 1846, just before the Moores arrived, more than 60 Americans lived at Branciforte or were scattered here and there among some 20 outlying ranchos. Business was conducted in the mercantile part of town where imported and locally produced goods were bought and sold. Doctors and midwives and extra work hands were hired. News, and matters of politics, power, and wealth were exchanged inside and outside of a saloon's swinging doors. And all in a mixed patois of languages: Spanish; English; Russian; and Portuguese.

Life could be fun, too. The Californios were widely known to be superb horsemen and horsewomen. They loved horseracing and other public spectacles so much, when there wasn't a rodeo going on at one of the ranchos they'd spend whole days in Santa Cruz at its mile-long racetrack or at the bull-and-bear-fight arena. Church festivals, marriages and births were celebrated lavishly. Sometimes the preparations and entertainment went on for weeks as a welcome diversion for the many families living on the ranchos where they might rarely see a visitor for months on end.

The foreigners either embraced this lifestyle or kept themselves apart according to their nature and their upbringing. Many of the Americans in Santa Cruz were culturally at odds with the native-born Californians. To them, an attitude that tried to balance pleasure with achievement simply meant lost opportunity. The best among the Americans emphasized the virtues of hard work, individual initiative, and obedience to what they may have called duty. Given the prevailing attitude of the time, the Americans felt this duty was to transform these wild lands and people into "civilized" versions of themselves and their notions of an orderly universe.

Isaac Graham exemplified one extreme of this American point of view. Born in 1800 in Virginia and raised in Kentucky, he'd been a full-time trapper and Indian fighter, was present at the death of Daniel Boone, and had run all over the Southwest and parts of California with Kit Carson. After years of trapping and hunting, he settled down in California in 1836.

Graham openly despised the native way of life and refused to become a Mexican citizen. A hard-drinking, hard-fighting man, he attracted a following among some of the other American immigrants who came over the Santa Fe Trail in the 1830s. A "colony" of these rough men collected at his place in the Pajaro Valley where he raised horses and cattle, ran a distillery and sold whiskey to seamen and trappers and any other desperados needing fortitude before trekking off into the wilderness. These were the men who followed Graham in his six-year career as a revolutionist that had ended, for him, in a Mexico City jail.

Released from prison through the intervention of friends and American military, Graham was paid a handsome indemnity of $36,000 for the troubles and humiliation he'd suffered. He returned and moved to the Santa Cruz hills in 1842.

He bought Rancho Zayante from his friend Joseph Ladd Majors, a road companion of his when he'd first come to Alta California in the early 1830's on the Santa Fe Trail. Majors had assimilated where Graham had not; the owner of Zayante was a naturalized citizen and married to a daughter of the prestigious Castro family. Since he wasn't a Mexican citizen, Graham could not purchase land from the Mexican government, but he could and did purchase Zayante from Majors. (It happened so quickly after Majors himself bought Zayante, it's tempting to think their deal might have been pre-arranged.) Graham built the first power saw in the area and a road for hauling lumber that is still in use today (Graham Hill Road), set up another distillery, and continued to raise cattle. Zayante was a major moneymaker. By selling hides, lumber and whiskey, Graham was worth a jaw-dropping $25,000 by 1850 when the Moores arrived.

Among other foreigners living at Branciforte who'd adapted more gracefully into Mexican life than Graham was Don José Antonio Bolcoff. In 1815 the 19-year-old Kamchatka native deserted a Russian ship as it was engaged in otter hunting and contraband trading while visiting Monterey. Bolcoff liked Monterey and plunged into re-invent-ing his life. Two years later his Orthodox baptism was ratified and he was accepted into the Roman Catholic Church. In 1822 he married 15-year-old María Candida Castro y Amador, a daughter of Don Joaquin Castro. In so doing he joined one of Alta California's oldest, most prominent Spanish families, and soon became a naturalized citizen.

When Bolcoff met his contemporary, Eli Moore, 25 years later, he was a man of influence and considerable substance in Santa Cruz. He'd served twice as the alcalde at the Branciforte presidio and from 1839 he was the man in charge at Mission Santa Cruz. In 1841 he was granted 12,147 acres of land called Rancho Refugio. As if that weren't enough, Bolcoff and his sons then got in on the Gold Rush early and made a fortune in mining. By the age of 50 Bolcoff had transformed himself from the young fugitive he once was to a solid citizen worth $8,000, a major landowner, an influential politician, and the father of 15 children.

First Native Son

The end of the Moores' journey marked the end of a very long year for Adaline. Installed in the Bolcoff adobe for scarcely a month, she gave birth to their first child, Eli Daniel Moore, on December 12, 1847, no doubt with the help of her mother- and sisters-in-law. All that training in the large family of her girlhood had paid off. Adaline had carried her child across the Plains and over mountains, been shuttled from place to place, faced danger and discomfort as the year wore on without any certainty of knowing when or if she would finally land in a place with a roof over her head. But now she'd made herself proud, having endured all to produce the first boy born to American parents on record in that part of California.

The two Moore households—Alexander's and Eli's—weathered the winter and became acquainted with the social dynamics in town. In the following May Alexander went into the milling business with José Bolcoff. Then the gold fever broke out and all help deserted the mill, leaving them flat. There wasn't much else for Alexander to do but to go, too. For the next year and a half he mined in sporadic bursts through Calaveras and Amador counties, prospecting as far as the Bear River; later he worked the American River and the Tuolumne. But in the end he wasn't much better off than when he'd started.

He returned to the Santa Cruz area for good in June of 1849 to find Adaline nursing their newest 3-month-old son. Alexander named him Joseph Ladd Majors in honor of Isaac Graham's great friend and ally. Maybe Alexander was being prescient, too—Majors would become treasurer of Santa Cruz County a year or so later—and hoped good fortune would rub off on his boy.

Alexander set his mind to finish building the sawmill on the Bolcoff ranch and with his father's help it was done by early August. He stayed on doing millwork at the ranch and in partnership with three associates accepted a contract supplying timber that was used to construct the Meiggs whaling wharf in San Francisco. The contract brought in as much as $2,000 per month for the timber and $12 a day for the paid hands.

Alexander turned to farming fulltime in 1852. In his memoir, Alexander says that the equipment they used were considered wonderful inventions by the native residents: especially the steel plow manufactured in Peoria, Illinois and a grain cradle, both of which the family had brought by the sheer strength of will power across the Plains with them from Missouri.

But they didn't have a threshing machine. When their first wheat crop came in they collected the sheaves of cut grain into huge piles, and gathered a herd of about 150 wild horses and colts with

---

Below: *The spirit of cooperation so evident in the Moores' early years in California endures for generations. Below, William Moore (Alex and Adaline's son) and a thrashing crew harvest hay on the Pescadero ranch. The original sepia-toned photograph was taken by George Franzen, of San Francisco, in about 1900.*

"a lot of vaqueros to drive and curse them back and forth over the grain until it was thrashed." Using shovels made of locally milled redwood they threw the "thrashed" grain up against the wind to blow away the chaff. Indians they hired then swept and gathered up the harvested grain.

Alexander bought land in Santa Cruz where the lighthouse now stands and moved his family to live there. A third child, Mary Rebecca, was born in September 1850, but she only lived 10 days. The Moores had better luck with the next baby, their third son, William Alexander Moore, who was born late in July 1851. That year marked another turning point in Alexander's fortunes.

Santa Cruz in 1850 was an energetic and ambitious place where men outnumbered women by about two to one. The town was growing so rapidly since the onset of the gold fever and California statehood that Americans who'd only recently arrived could jump straight to the top level of local society without stopping to count their money. Aflame with dreams to conquer their personal destinies, these men formed and dissolved alliances with each other at the drop of a coin.

Everybody knew everybody else and what they were doing almost before they knew it themselves. When a new house went up everyone was alert to all details, from the wedding guest list of the couple that would move into the house to the source of the lumber used to build it. Such was the case with the beautiful home being built on Sylvar Street for Sheriff Francisco Alzina—Santa Cruz County's first 'lawman'—and María Gonzàles. The lumber to build María's house was brought down the coast from her father's rancho in the northern frontier section of Santa Cruz County, a place called Rancho Pescadero.

Eli Moore had heard a lot about María's father, another leading figure in the Santa Cruz political arena named Don Juan José Gonzàles. He'd also heard about the rolling grasslands and redwood timber forests of Gonzàles's Rancho Pescadero from his friend, Isaac Graham. Graham had just started construction of a house at Rancho Punta del Año Nuevo several miles south of Pescadero that he'd picked up at a sheriff's sale. Graham no doubt sang its praises. Eli realized that, beyond New Year's Point, getting to Pescadero wouldn't be easy but its very remoteness might even have increased its appeal for him. He and his sons, Alexander and Thomas, got on their horses and rode off to see what the country had to offer.

Pescadero was the ultimate for Alexander. When he saw it, he knew at once he wanted to live out the rest of his days in that place where "the grain grew as high as a horse's back."

In a few years the town the Moores dreamed of would materialize at Pescadero. An arrow indicates the possible site of the original Gonzàles adobe.

Noel William Dias Collection.

Rancho Pescadero 1833 – 1852 and beyond

"They settled in Santa Cruz first; then they came up here and bought a Spanish grant. They sold [portions of] it to a lot of other people—the Weekses, for one, and Alexander's brother, Tom Moore. They needed people to work, [in] those days ... not like now [when] we have too many people ... because everything was by hand. No tractors, horses, and milkers, you know—they [needed] a number of people.

"[The Moores] were into farming. They lived in Juan José Gonzàles's [adobe] house while they built their home spot up here at the Phipps's vegetable stand. ...

"[At that time there] were just Indians and Juan José Gonzàles [living here], [and] whoever he had in here working for him. There are signs of Indian relics along the creeks. I've seen them. A couple of bowls out back my father picked up somewhere, with I don't know what you call the round rock that you grind stuff with—a round rock like a bowl and then a thing you beat it with…a mortar and pestle. That's about it, as far as people being here. They were a hardy bunch of people who came across the Plains in a covered wagon."

— Clifford Moore, 2003

Don Juan José Gonzàles

Juan José Gonzàles was born at the Yerba Buena (San Francisco) presidio in 1805, the son of Don Francisco Gonzàles, a Spaniard from Mexico who was an officer in the Mexican Army, and María Tomasa Peralta, a first-generation Californian. Juan José grew up in a military milieu and is reputed to have been a soldier himself at the San Francisco presidio in 1822-23.

Don Juan inherited his father's cattle brand when he was 16 years old and registered it in Santa Cruz. This may have signified that he was ready to assume a man's responsibilities for in that year, 1821, Juan José married 20-year-old María Ana de Jesús Rodriguèz. This was a great coup in itself. Ana de Jesús was the daughter of José Antonio Rodriguèz, one of the original Spanish pioneers who had come to San Gabriel, Alta California in 1787, an officer in the Army of Spain. In 1798, when he was in his mid-thirties, Rodriguèz got to Branciforte with his large and growing family and served out the rest of his military career there. As Leon Rowland says of Joaquin Castro and José Antonio Rodriguèz in his book, *Annals of Santa Cruz*, "Two score years later their sons and daughters were to

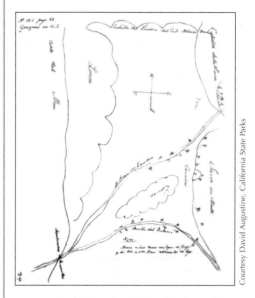

Left, Juan José Gonzàles's cattle brand, which he inherited from his father. Above is the map (No. 181 page 88, Gonzàles vs. US) of Rancho Pescadero, granted to Gonzàles in 1833. The boundaries were imprecise, which later caused troubles when portions of the original grant were sold to American buyers, and the terms used are not in modern Spanish. Note the interesting name of the east boundary—"Boundary of the Moon"—and that the designation for the eastern hills indicates they are forested.

own a quarter of a million acres in what is now Santa Cruz County. Their children were the aristocrats of Branciforte."

In 1833, not long after his father's death, Juan Gonzàles was granted 3,282 acres of land called Rancho San Antonio, or Rancho Pescadero (The Fishing Place) by Governor José Figueroa. At one time the Spanish padres had planned to establish a mission at Pescadero. The site was 40 miles or so north of Santa Cruz on the coast route to Mission Dolores at Yerba Buena, a perfect place to stop and rest where the trail crossed a stream. From its source 25 miles up in the hills, the healthy creek full of salmon and steelhead threaded its way through a sheltered alluvial valley to the ocean. Wild game, fish, sea otters, and wild fowl were abundant and the soil was fertile.

But the trail up the coast deteriorated soon after leaving Santa Cruz. It narrowed down to a path choked by poison oak and scrub brush; skirted the edges of steep cliffs that crumbled into the surf; and sank in the sand on beaches constantly reshaped by mutable tides. Moving supplies and passengers in wagons or carriages was a daunting proposition. The padres' plan languished and died.

The Branciforte mission was secularized the year following Gonzàles's receipt of the grant and he took on other responsibilities before he could move to the Pescadero land. Gonzàles was appointed mayordomo when the previous comisario—his father-in-law, José Antonio Rodriguèz—retired after 30 years on the job. Now the 29-year-old Gonzàles was a family man with six children—five girls and one boy. He owned land and cattle

Moore & DePue's Illustrated History of San Mateo County – 1878.

30   Portraits of Pescadero

and was solidly connected with the oldest and most powerful families at the Santa Cruz pueblo.

His star continued to rise. In 1836 Gonzàles was given a captain's commission in Alvarado's new militia and became known as a "freedom fighter." Together with a man named Pinta he organized a body of 35 men and boys and went down to Los Angeles with Alvarado, Castro, and Graham to help them negotiate with the stubborn southerners. He distinguished himself by his actions in the fights that ensued and when a compromise was reached, he returned home more solidly entrenched in Santa Cruz politics than ever.

Gonzàles spent most of his time in Santa Cruz, and not very much time himself at Rancho Pescadero where he'd installed an overseer (José Antonio Castro and his family) to occupy the land on his behalf. But an incident occurred in 1841 to shift his attention while he was acting as the Juez de Paz (Justice of the Peace).

Acting on Gonzàles's orders, Gil Sanchez, the tithe collector, shot and killed one of the Robles boys. The Robles were generally known to be thoroughly unsavory characters and were not popular in Santa Cruz, but the Monterey authorities reprimanded both Gonzàles and Sanchez by exiling them from Branciforte for a period of one year. Gonzàles probably retreated to his rancho in Pescadero for the duration—a pretty safe bet, judging by the name of his daughter, María Simona del Refugio, born a year later. In 1842 Gonzàles is presumed to have been living with his wife and at least some of their 11 or 12 children in a small adobe dwelling set on the bank of Pescadero Creek at the north end of the present town.

With his wife and family installed at Pescadero, Gonzàles continued to keep a foot planted in Santa Cruz. When California became the 31st state of the Union on September 9, 1850, the first election in Santa Cruz showed these Pescadero names on the roster: Thomas [Jefferson] Weeks; Don Juan Gonzàles; Alexander Moore; and Eli Moore. (Eli ran for county judge but was not elected). Santa Cruz County was formed the following year and Gonzàles was definitely back in favor, filling the important post of Juez de Campo (inspector of cattle brands and arbiter of title to roving livestock).

Eli Moore obviously knew Gonzàles well enough to see that Gonzàles's interests in Santa Cruz might be more absorbing than were his interests in managing an isolated rancho full-time. Like most other Californios after the Americans took over, Gonzàles was very likely land-rich and cash-poor. Even though Gonzàles was building a new adobe at Pescadero in anticipation of his moving there on a more permanent basis, he might still be disposed to unloading some of his property. Eli exercised his powers of persuasion and paid $6,000

Above: *John Tuffly's feed mill.*

Opposite: *Barzillai Hayward's spread four miles upstream from town on the Pescadero Creek is a splendid example of the kind of enterprise shown by the early pioneers. Logging was a major industry in the early days; Hayward was one of the original settlers who arrived in Pescadero around 1856 whose business thrived. Although the mill is long gone its general location is marked today by a heritage cypress tree—over 250 years old—standing on Pescadero Creek road near the bridge crossing.*

Above: *This is the earliest photograph we have of Pescadero town. The orchard—of white- and red-blooming cherry, apple, and pear trees—house, and barn belonged to Braddock Weeks, one of the earliest settlers in Pescadero. The house—built between 1856 and 1860—does not yet show the porch and ornamentation that were added later.*

Opposite page: *Alexander Moore's spread, with its beautiful house, as it appeared in the early days.*
The house burned down in the mid-1970s from a fire set by vandals.

to Gonzàles and his wife for a portion of Rancho Pescadero on September 15, 1852.

Gonzàles died before he could realize his plan of retiring to Rancho Pescadero. According to an 1856 article in a Santa Cruz newspaper, Gonzàles had been living in Pescadero from 1833 to the time of his death in 1854. There are discrepancies as to the actual events surrounding his death, as well as to the date. According to one source, he died on March 6, 1853, "soon after a drunken carousal." If this is true, we can only hope it was a great party.

A TOWN IS BORN

A little over five years had passed since Alexander had refused Weber's offer of "a mile square" at Stockton. Now he had a second chance. Adaline delivered her fifth baby George on March 5, 1853 in Santa Cruz. Ten days later Alexander and his brother Thomas moved to Pescadero with enough of their belongings to set up a base; Adaline and their children would come later. Alexander started construction of the first frame house in Pescadero on his portion of the land grant his father had purchased. The lumber had to be hauled from the mill in Santa Cruz by oxen, pulling the load at low tide over the wet sand at Waddell Creek. When finished in 1855, it was a fine, 14-room farmhouse with a handsome covered

deck that wrapped around two sides.

The records strongly suggest that the Moores and several of their friends in Santa Cruz came to Pescadero with the *intention* to found a town settlement. According to the *History of San Mateo County — 1883* the first white settlers arrived in Pescadero in January 1853, a couple of months in advance of the Moores' move. They were Richard Vestal, Henry Ryan, Jonathan Rader and Joshua Poole. Ryan and Vestal leased part of the land that Eli Moore retained, and Poole rented a piece of the Gonzàles rancho.

Rader, a 30-year-old Virginia native, and Poole, a 28-year-old lawyer from Indiana, were based in Santa Cruz and well acquainted with the Moores. Jonathan Rader had been living in Adaline Moore's household with her children and a third adult since at least 1850, while Alexander was listed as living separately in his father's house. Although this may or may not literally have been the case, the public record raises questions as to the nature of Rader's relationship with Adaline. But people were very practical in those days. Given Adaline's moral upbringing, the fact that she was pregnant and Alexander away during most of this time, Rader's presence in Adaline's household may have been meant to provide greater security for her while she was alone. Alexander's trust in Rader is evident in that he rented property to him when Rader came to Pescadero, further suggesting that Rader actually was *sent* there as an advance point man on the Moores' behalf.

Another American with ideas of establishing a town in Pescadero appeared on the scene in the same year. The Moores had become acquainted with San Francisco lawyer James Brennen when they purchased the land from Juan José Gonzàles; Brennen had done some work for Gonzàles, for which Gonzàles was in arrears paying him. The Moores were sympathetic to their fellow American and might have worked out a deal of their own with the lawyer; or Brennen may have jumped at the possibility of a new venture by aligning himself with the Moores. In 1853 Brennen hired a surveyor

The Moore Family

named Lucius F. Cooper—probably another man with whom the Moores were well acquainted—to lay out a map with lot numbers for the town of Pescadero. A year later, Brennen paid about $2,400 to Doña María Ana de Jesus Gonzàles for the "downtown area" and began selling lots.

More of the founding families of Pescadero town arrived in 1854, again through the Santa Cruz connection. One of Santa Cruz resident Thomas Jefferson Weeks' brothers, Braddock Weeks, had gone into partnership with his newly arrived cousin Lafayette Chandler running a dairy ranch. Three years later 21-year-old Chandler broke off on his own to farm 171 acres called "Level Lea." A third Weeks brother, Bartlett Varnum Weeks, moved to Pescadero in 1858.

The lumber industry was heating up in those years and the thickly forested hills around San Gregorio and Pescadero were especially rich with thousand-year-old redwoods and oak. John Tuffly drove a herd of cattle up from Santa Cruz for Alexander Moore, but didn't come back to live in Pescadero until 1856 when he set up the first grist- and sawmill four miles east of town on Pescadero Creek. August Blomquist, the patriarch of an immigrant family from Sweden, set up another water-powered saw that year and was operating his shingle mill at McCormick Creek on the lower Pescadero. John Beeding came with three other men in 1854; he settled on the creek below Barzillai Hayward's mill and lived there until his death by suicide some years later. John Pence, one of Beeding's companions, died the same year that they moved to Pescadero. His was the first death of a white man recorded at Pescadero and he was buried "on a mound at the end of San Gregorio Street, with a fence placed around it by the hands of strangers." Henry Wurr, a German immigrant who worked timber upstream in Harrison [Loma Mar], is also recorded as a settler in 1856.

The "downtown area" of Pescadero was taking shape. John Beeson started a blacksmith shop.

Besides Thomas Moore and his wife, and the Alexander Moores, other family names that appeared in the 1860 census are familiar: Henry Wheeler, a Massachusetts-born man; George, Lafitte (Lafayette) and Soffitte Chandler; John Moore, from France; and a Williams. They were blacksmiths, mill workers, farmers, lighthouse-keepers, dairy ranchers, laborers, and barkeeps. Many of the Portuguese named were whalers who lived at Punta de Ballena [Pigeon Point].

In the fall of 1856 Samuel Bean opened the first hotel in a newly-finished building erected by Samuel Besse, Jon Rader and Braddock Weeks. Five years later, in 1861, capitalist Loren Coburn took over as its proprietor. The establishment passed into other hands in 1863 when Charles Swanton and his wife, Sarah Washburn, established what was to become Pescadero's signature resort, The Swanton Hotel.

In 1855 the first mercantile store was a little shake building run by a man named Downes, but he didn't last longer than a year. Samuel Besse, Braddock Weeks, and Jon Rader took over as proprietors; in a couple years' time, Besse and Weeks had tired of the venture and left it all to Rader. He moved the store to the north side of the creek in 1858 but apparently couldn't make a go of it alone; he sold it to H.C. Bidwell and another partner. By 1860 Samuel Besse was back, this time in partnership with John Garretson, a New Jersey blacksmith who'd been in town for about a year.

Rader disappears from Pescadero accounts soon after he sold his interest in the store. The reason why might be illuminated by the following story found in the *History of San Mateo County – 1883*:

"[1856:] This year a justice of the peace was elected, and it is said that during his whole official term, he was called upon but once to exercise his magisterial functions, and that was in the preliminary examination of a man charged with murder.

"… On the night of February 2, 1857, a man

Top: *Western Union and Wells Fargo Bank offices, housed in a building at the southwest corner of early Pescadero's central crossroads, with mule-team wagons and buggies drawn up. 1880s or even earlier.*

Above: *The I.R. Goodspeed General Merchandise store. The sign on the roof of the Lincoln Livery Stable at far right advertises "Saddle horses & carriages to hire cheap." 1860–'70.*

named Richard Jones, better known as 'Little Dick,' in company with others, was gambling at the store of Rader, Besse & Weeks. Sometime during the night Jones left, but returned again about daylight and knocked at the door for admission. The parties inside refused to let him in, and in his rage he kicked a hole through the side of the store, which was an old shake building…. Rader picked up a shotgun, and going to the door killed 'Little Dick' in his tracks.

"Another one of the party in the store at the time, named Long, was arrested for the shooting…. The justice held Long to answer. Rader, however, appeared before the grand jury and confessed that it was he who killed 'Little Dick.' Long, of course, was discharged, and Rader was tried and acquitted … ."

In 1857 Alexander built the first schoolhouse in Pescadero in a corner of his orchard just north of his house. The building was 14 ft. x 16 ft. He hired a former governess from Isaac Graham's household, Mrs. Shield Knight, as a teacher and paid her a salary of $40 a month out of his own pocket. Counting his own and a few Spanish children, there were seven students.

Two years later a man named Sam Merit took charge of the school as its principal. In a 1973 interview, Louise Moore Williamson remembered a story her father, Walter Henry Moore, must have told her about his childhood in the late 1850's. The little schoolhouse used to get very cold in the winter; Merit wanted a stove to heat it but didn't have

Seated, left to right, are Alexander and Adaline Moore; daughter Ida Jane Moore; and son David Moore. Standing, left to right, are Bill (William) Moore, Joe (Joseph Ladd Majors) Moore; Walter Henry Moore and oldest son, Eli Daniel Moore.

much money. One day he went downtown to the Besse & Garretson store where such things were sold and told the proprietor his story. Isaac R. Goodspeed, "a long, lean young man" so fresh out of medical school he had only 25 cents in his pocket, overheard Merit and made him a bet. If the principal could carry the stove on his back from where they stood to the school without once putting it down, Garretson would give it to him as a contribution to local education. Schoolhouse Hill, near Alexander Moore's home, was about a mile from town, but Merit accepted the wager. Hoisting the stove onto his back, he started walking. Goodspeed walked along with him to make sure he never once let the stove touch the ground. The teacher carried his burden without dropping it and won the bet.

Dr. Goodspeed was doubly pleased with this turn of events because soon afterwards he himself was hired to teach in the little building as Merit's successor. In a little while the doctor was elected Justice of the Peace and "he divided his time between meting out justice to sinners, healing the sick, and instilling knowledge into the young mind." He lived in Pescadero for 10 years before moving away to San Mateo.

Alexander Moore recalls in his memoir, *A Pioneer of '47*, that they had "no word and little communication" with the rest of the world back in the 1850s. The first settlers paid Sebastian Armas $3 to ride to Searsville—a lively logging town that had popped up like an early spring mushroom near the present junction of Portola and Old La Honda roads—for the mail and bring it back the same day; Armas made this trip once a week.

Alex raised some cattle and farmed potatoes, filling every bag with 5 or 6 pounds. In this way he made more money off the Gold Rush than he had ever done by mining; potatoes shipped well and were much in demand in the San Francisco markets that supplied the Argonauts. To supplement their table the family had their own kitchen garden and an orchard, and the whole of Pescadero's dairy and cattle raising industry. Hunting and fishing added variety to their diet as well as providing gentlemen with amusement and an occasional test of skill. Louise Williamson says that Alexander enjoyed a reputation for being a very good shot. Whenever he went deer hunting he never took more than three shells with him.

Adaline's career as a mother continued on as it had in Santa Cruz, but now she had no women friends close by who could help her and share her personal challenges. The family had been in

"My grandmother [Adaline Moore] was a midwife and used to take my father [Walter Henry Moore] on horseback to Santa Cruz where she had to confine a woman. I had a gold buckle in the safe deposit box that was mined by a fellow and had a gold buckle made to give to my grandmother for confining his wife. But it was of such soft gold that it wore through and had to be filled."

— Louise Moore Williamson

Pescadero for only a little over a year when, pregnant again, she got on her horse and rode back to Santa Cruz where she could give birth comforted by known and loving hands. John Eli Moore was born there on May 20, 1854. Both John and his closest older brother, George, were two more of Adaline's babies that would be lost to her. They died before they reached manhood: George, at age 12; and John, at 13. There are no records yet found that can tell us why or how Baby Mary, George, and John died but, as testament to her fortitude, Adaline triumphed again when she bore the Moores' seventh child and only living girl, Ida Jane Moore, on May 28, 1856 in Pescadero. David Eugene Moore followed two years later, on March

26, 1858. Still game, Adaline went for nine. Nearly 42 years old, she gave birth to her last baby, Walter Henry Moore, on June 14, 1864, and then she quit.

Finished with bearing and birthing children herself, Adaline transformed her knowledge and considerable experience of it into a career as a midwife. Her indomitable energy and her willingness to help old friends shows how strongly she must have felt about kindnesses paid to her in the past by the small society of women who had pioneered the Far West Coast alongside their men.

By 1860, Pescadero had a population of 428 people. In the span of just 13 years Alexander and Adaline Moore had said goodbye to one life, crossed prairies and mountains, and helped build a town. They'd created a new life, one that would endure for another four generations in this sweet, quiet little place.

Above: *The Moores at their family home in Pescadero. Adaline and Alexander Moore are seated in front with their grandchildren, Ida and James Alexander ("Alec"). Standing, from left to right, are Dave Moore; Hattie and Bill Moore; Frances and Walter Moore. Ca. 1892.*

Inset left: *Ida Moore, Walter Henry Moore's daughter.*
Inset right: *James Alexander "Alec" Moore, William Moore's son.*

Ever Since 1853

Third and Fourth Generations

James Alexander ("Alec") Moore was born December 12, 1888, the only child of William Moore (everyone in town called him "Uncle Bill") and Hattie Huff. They had waited five years after marrying to get him and they raised their only child with warm attention. Alec grew up in a small house that was close by to his grandparents' larger spread and within easy walking distance of Pescadero's main street. He was as familiar with horses and dairy cattle, with growing crops in the fields, as he was with his mother's sugar cookies. It was a simple but satisfying life.

From the time he was a small kid, Alec knew he belonged on a horse's back, just like his grandfather Alex. He learned to read the signs written on the land as he rode herd, learned when to plant and when to harvest, plus the whole life cycle and business of dairy cows. He was 12 when his grandparents—first Adaline and later in the year Alexander Moore—died in 1902. Alec was 15 when the San Francisco earthquake of 1906 occurred; about 10 years later he enlisted in the Army, put on a uniform, and sat for a photograph with his cousin, Walter, before going to serve in the First World War. LaVerne Brazil says in her monograph that Alec's father, Bill Moore, was a veteran of the Great War as well, serving in France. If this is true, the old man was formidable, as he would have enlisted at the already venerable age of 66!

Left: *Alec was comfortable on his horse, Nig, from boyhood.*
Below: *Alec and Nig in front of the barn on the Moore Ranch, early 1890's. It stands to this day, still in use as a working barn.*

When Alec was 33 he gave up life as a dashing young blade to marry Annie Cabral, a woman from an old-time local family living in the Pomponio. Her father was a sheepherder, "tending sheep for people all over the country, clear up into Nevada." There were no fences in those days and since he had to go wherever the sheep migrated, Mr. Cabral wasn't around much—according to Alec's daughter-in-law, Ruth Moore, just long enough to come home and get his wife pregnant before taking off again. His methods were apparently effective. There were three boys—Jack, Bernard, and Joe—and two girls—Annie and her younger sister Marie.

Annie had gentle dark eyes that lit up when she smiled and a get-it-done, independent approach to life. Annie also had a daughter from a previous marriage, Dora Goularte. When Alec and Annie had their own son, Clifford, born in May 1933, Dora was not living with them, so Clifford grew up as an only child just like his Dad.

Although young Clifford didn't have his paternal grandfather around for too many years before he died, "Uncle Bill" Moore had a big influence on the boy's character.

"We lived up by the barn and [my grandparents] lived not too far down by the road on the same ranch. I used to be kind of an ornery little soul, I guess [laughs]. My grandfather used to take me downtown and if I'd cuss good enough for him, he'd let me have a cigar! [laughs] You might be walking by and I might tell you what I thought of you [laughs] whether I knew you or not!

"[My grandmother] was just a good old soul. She hardly ever went anywhere and grandfather always walked the town or rode a horse or whatever. They never owned a car, I don't think."

It was the Depression. Clifford's folks, like most everyone else in Pescadero, didn't have much money. They made up for it by falling back on their own resources and working hard. If they needed something they couldn't buy, they'd find a way to invent it.

Left, top: *Cousins Walter Harold Moore, seated in the chair, and Alec Moore sit for a formal portrait in their military uniforms. Ca. 1917.*
Middle: *Friends, left to right, Andrew Pico; Charlie Steele Jr.; Alec and Walter Moore. 1915.*
Lower: *Alec Moore and his dog Spot at home. His mother Hattie Huff Moore is on the porch. March 5, 1919.*

"We used to have little things we made. Airplanes and things out of balsa wood. Used to play with little soldiers. I knew where the black powder was and I used to make little bombs and blow them off, and so forth and so on. [laughs]

"I got a red wagon one Christmas, when I was about five or six. My father and his milker went out, took a sled that they could pack, and put sled marks through the yard; then it was [as if] the reindeer took it over the fence and that's the last you ever saw of the sled. That was the sleigh, see? [They] put the marks [to show] that Santa had been there; then they picked up [the sled] and put it back where it belonged, that Santa took off."

"My folks were just common people. Mom was a hairdresser and beautician, a housewife. [I] remember her having a little shop and having people come in; she had to have a little pocket money, too, you know. Doing a thing on the side. You didn't have to have a license or anything in those days, you just did it. [She] did the cooking, and took care of things. Used to have a Chevy and she'd go out shopping once in a great while.

"My Dad was a dairyman, a farmer. He broke horses. I still have the bill of sale for his saddle—made in 1913—the chaps, and everything. I think it was $55, which was a lot of money at that time. And he did crop surveying for the agriculture department. A guy would say, 'I got 20 acres of peas,' and he'd have to go survey it and see if there were 20 acres of peas. (They had some type of a subsidy going in them days.)

"They were not rich people. They barely made a living is what it amounted to. We didn't live real fancy.

"… The old-timers did a lot of hunting—deer hunting, quail, rabbit hunting—during the Depression. That's the way a lot of them lived. You had to have something to put on the table. I can remember Dad talking…he had dairy cattle at the time and people used to buy the steer calves—bull calves—and you got a few bucks out of them, but when the Depression hit you couldn't give them away. You had to hit them in the head with a hammer and throw them in the gulch because you could only eat so many and you couldn't get rid of them.

"My Dad had a struggle. He lived, but they had their own garden; they had their own milk; refrigeration was just coming into being, so you had coolers. Not any prepared foods. They went fishing, ate fish; they went hunting, ate deer; had fowl, ducks, and geese…. My Dad was an avid hunter. [It was] a different way of life. It was a little tough for some of the people."

The first car Alec Moore had was a Model A Ford. He would drive it to Santa Cruz to pick up supplies for the animals or to Redwood City on business; regular shopping was done in town. Clifford remarks that the system in Pescadero worked so that the

Annie Cabral, below, and Alec Moore, bottom. *Alec often would model for post card photographs, such as this one, but he was the genuine article.*

"*My father was a very honest man. He had a strong character.*"

The Moore Family 41

Above left: *Alec and Annie Moore with their newborn, Cliff, and "Uncle Bill" Moore, Cliff's grandfather. 1933.* Above right: *Cliff plays with one of his second cousins in the yard at Constable Walter Moore's house in Pescadero town.* Right: *Clifford, during his career as a Boy Scout.*

"*I had this dog, Tip. He was smarter than I was, he wouldn't let me out in the street. Little guy would want to get in the street and he'd just get in front of me, walk back and forth; I'd pound on his back, but he still wouldn't let me out in the street.*"

---

farmers basically got paid once a year; dairymen were a little different. They held charge accounts at Williamson's store and paid for it when they got their money.

Money figured in the Moore household in a very personal way, too. Alec Moore was the Treasurer for the Native Sons and held the money for the rodeos they used to have at the Shade Ranch. (Today, Clifford carries on the tradition by serving as Treasurer for the Native Sons.)

"*Rodeos were a big thing in the early days. The first one they had where Shade Ranch is. No buildings or nothing. They plowed alongside the hill and made furrows—that was the seats.*

"*[My Dad] was very involved in the rodeo. There was a dance and they had the rodeo on the Sunday. They had canteens and entry fees and since he was treasurer, they'd bring all the money to him. He'd throw it in an old ten-gallon milk can and it'd be $3500 to $5000. That's quite a bit of money in those days, you know. He'd take the milk can up to the barn and bury it in the hay. The bank wasn't open and if anybody got wind that he had that money, he'd say—'I don't know where it is. It's up in the barn in the hay.' [chuckles] They'd come Monday night and scatter it all over the floor—nickels, dimes, quarters and dollar bills; five dollar bills; the whole pile—and get everything segregated, then count it all and then they'd go to the bank with it Tuesday. Bank of America at that time. That was the original bank in town.*"

As a young man, Clifford had a keen interest in motorcyles. He remembers when his father's cousin, Walter Moore, was the constable in Pescadero and he would "threaten" to get Cliff with his motorcycle. "I'd let off of it when I'd go to make the turn off the bridge and it would backfire at two o'clock in the morning. He wasn't too appreciative of it."

LUCKY YOU LIVE PESCADERO

When Clifford was a teenager his folks got a divorce. He doesn't know why. "I guess she got tired of living here and she just moved away to Santa Cruz. My Dad never did remarry." Alec Moore continued to live on at the home ranch, doing much as he had always done, work, and seeing his son Clifford go through high school, get a job off the ranch, serve in the Army, and come home to get married himself.

The town was changing as different generations grew up and went away; many did not return. As kids went away, the labor force shifted too. Cliff remembers during the '40s and '50s the workers were mostly Filipino; they lent what he thought was a colorful note to the local mix.

"The labor force at one time was Filipino here on the Coast. I used to like to listen to them talk; they have a little 'sing' to their vocabulary. When I was a kid growing up I went over one time to this ranch where they were having a big thing, a cock fight, and I said, 'Let's go.' I saw more money lying around there on the floor than I ever seen in Reno, for Chrissake. All them guys saved all their money and they were serious gamblers. [laughs] I didn't know what kind of games they were playing. They were Filipino games, you know. They had the cock fights going on there—very illegal, but you'd get wind of it, you'd go see what was going on! [laughs]"

As the years went by Cliff and his wife, Ruth, were able to find a place to buy in Pescadero. In 1967 they built the house they live in today, across the road from where Alexander and Adaline Moore raised Pescadero's first frame house (destroyed by vandals in a January 1974 fire). For Cliff, finding housing to live in is one of the biggest problems young people (or anyone) faces if they want to stay here. He doesn't know what the next generation will be able to hold on to. And this problem is tied

Above: *Young Hattie Huff and William Alexander Moore, married April 9, 1883.*
Below: *Grandfather, "Uncle Bill," died when Cliff was three, but he had a big influence on the boy.*
Bottom: *Clifford and his half-sister Dora Goularte at the Moore Ranch barn. 1934.*

Top: *Josiah Caldwell Williamson, age 19, came from Massachusetts to California in 1869, and worked four years at a dairy south of Pescadero before hiring on as a clerk for P.G. Stryker, John Garretson, and then the Levy Brothers. In February 1885 he opened the doors to his own store.*

Above: *The main street of Pescadero in the early '20s had many more businesses in evidence than we see today. Fires in the mid-to-late-'20s destroyed most of the aging wood buildings that are seen in this picture.*

Above: *Cliff Moore is the boy in the striped shirt, top row, near center. Ca. 1940.*

in as well with the basic attitudes and relationships modern communities have toward the land itself, including absentee ownership.

"*Our county doesn't want any building over here whatsoever. They really want to keep it all for open space. We don't need any more open space. They don't know what the hell to do with what they got. It's too bad. The few cows I have here pay the taxes and upkeep but you couldn't make a living off of them.*

"*[In the past] all these hills were farmed around; looked nice. No brush. No weeds. If the weeds take over, we don't have a crop. And it helped keep down the fire hazard, too. I [learned from my father] how to take care of things, how to keep weeds off the ranch.... My people kept thistles off this place for a 100 years. It's gonna get to the point my place will get so many weeds on it now I'll have to give up trying to fight them, too.*

"*...This was a big lumbering community for San Francisco in the early days. They used to load the ships there at Pigeon Point. [People] talk [now] about how the trees grow up, and they don't want them cut—well, sooner or later everything grows old and dies. A redwood tree, you cut it off, it grows again. That's why they call it second growth. Second growth can grow so much faster than first growth because first growth struggles; [when] it's cut down, then second growth has got the root system and it grows real fast.*

"*Well, my theory of the whole thing is that the good Lord didn't put this land here just to look at. He put it here to be used, and for people to make a living off of. That's my theory. It's not just to look at; it's for use.*"

The town is smaller now than it used to be; and it's very slow-growing. But for people like Clifford Moore, whose ancestors gambled with their lives to create Pescadero town, they wouldn't want to live anyplace else. Why not?

"It's quiet," he says. "Nobody bothers you too much."

Sources

All photographs are from the Clifford James Moore Collection archived in the Pescadero Historical Society inventory unless otherwise noted.

Alexander, Philip W. — *History of San Mateo County*. Press of Burlingame Publishing Company; Burlingame, CA; 1916.

Beck, Warren A. and David A. Williams — *California, A History of the Golden State*. Doubleday & Company, Inc.; Garden City, NY; 1972.

Harrison, E.S. — *History of Santa Cruz County*. Pacific Press Publishing Co.; San Francisco, CA; 1892.

Hunt, Douglas L. (compiler) — *History and Genealogy of Jose Antonio Rodriguez (1754 – 1820), Soldado de Cuera for the King of Spain*. Portland, OR.

Koch, Margaret — *Santa Cruz County, Parade of the Past*. Valley Publishers, Fresno, CA; 1973.

Marschner, Janice — *California 1850, A Snapshot in Time*. Coleman Ranch Press, Sacramento, CA. February 2000.

McCloud, Roy Walter — *History of San Mateo County, California*; Vols. I and II. S.J. Clarke Pub. Co., Chicago, IL; 1928.

Rowland, Leon — *Santa Cruz, The Early Years*. Paper Vision Press, Santa Cruz, CA; 1980.

Spainhour, Irene Cooper (compiler) — *The Spainhour Family*. Lone Jack, MO; 1984.

Steele, Catherine B. and Wilfred H. Steele — *"The Steeles of Point Año Nuevo, A family genealogy and history from 1591 – 2000."*

California census of 1850; 1860; 1870. *Register of voters* for 1890; 1896; 1904; 1908; 1930.

Santa Cruz Census for 1850, by Mike Harvey.

The 1860 Census of Santa Cruz County California. Revised and compiled by D.D. Fletcher; B.D. Press. December 1997.

Interview with Clifford Moore and his wife, Ruth; July 15, 2003. Pescadero Historical Society.

Interview with Velia Garcia; Mexican History in Pescadero. September 17, 2003. Pescadero Historical Society.

Records from St. Arbogust Church, Muttenz Switzerland; Moravian Archives, Winston Salem, N.C.; The Eleven Volumes of Moravians in N.C.

San Mateo County History Museum Archives:

Brazil, Laverne — *"The Moore Family of Pescadero."* [961 SM] June 1948.

Cardoza, Verne — *"Old Spanish Families of the Coastside."* [SM 452] June 1942.

Oral histories of : Walter H. Moore; Louise Moore Williamson; Frank George. [78-218 Transcripts] 1973.

Personal letters including a list of burials at the Pioneer Cemetery overlooking the Alexander Moore home in Pescadero. [1610 MS].

Bancroft Library:

Charles Hopper and the Pilgrims of the Pacific; a 1841 California Pioneer, his narrative and other documents edited by Franklin Beard. Southern Mines Press, La Grange, CA; 1981.

Montgomery, R.T. — *Narrative of Charles Hopper, A California Pioneer of 1841*; written at Napa 1871.

Wichels, John — *A Brief Biographical Sketch of Charles Hopper—Hunter, Trapper, Explorer—One of the Early Pioneers of Yountville, Napa County*.

Hopper Guides California Wagon Train in 1847: (incl.) *Moore, Alexander, A pioneer of '47*; 1878.

Online:

Wikipedia and other online sources for states of Tennessee, Missouri, North Carolina; history of Moravians; Isaac Graham; Santa Cruz County.

A bull rider loses his grip in a Pescadero Rodeo event at the Shade Ranch. August 2, 1953.

The Weeks Family
Frances Bell Weeks

Frances Weeks (Dubel) in her home "office." April 21, 1996.

Born April 27, 1916 in Pescadero, Fannie Louise Weeks was a third-generation member of the Weeks family—one of the earliest to settle the town in the mid-1850s—the granddaughter of Bartlett and Annie Washburn Weeks and the oldest daughter of Edward and Hazel Bell Weeks' five children. She grew up in Pescadero in the historic house her grandfather built on what is now Goulson Street. Raised under the strict, stern authority of a father she remembers as being possessed by occasional bouts of temper, and her city-bred mother, who had her own high standards of how a young lady should turn out, Fannie's independent, bright-minded spirit often clashed against restraint. She left home in 1933 when she was 17 and changed her name to Frances Bell Weeks.

Frances escaped to Berkeley where she found lodgings and enrolled in a business college to learn accounting. She met a young man named John Wesley Dubel, fell in love, and married him. The couple eventually settled in Santa Cruz, but Frances kept in touch with Pescadero and her younger brother, Ed Weeks, who still lived in town. Although Frances entertained the idea of buying property in town at one time and expressed fond memories of her childhood home, she never did return for good.

At the end of her life Frances Dubel, a retired widow, lived in a small, comfortable house near the ocean in Santa Cruz, several blocks away from her daughter, Ruth Dubel Ditty. In spite of various physical ailments Frances still drove her own car to doctor and hair appointments and did her own shopping. She spent many happy hours at her home computer, translating texts into Braille with the use of a specialized keyboard, and doing research on her favorite subjects of genealogy and history. Days after our first and only interview with her she died suddenly on April 8, 2003, but the stories she told in the few hours we spent together add immeasurable flavor and life to the portraits of people and Pescadero from a century ago.

The Pioneer Generation

Starting in the late 1840s four brothers named Weeks and two of their first cousins named Chandler set sail from their home in Maine to make the hellish voyage to the California Coast. Although there are two branches of the Weeks family from Maine recorded to be in the Pescadero area in the mid-nineteenth century, the Weeks who pioneered the town's settlement—arriving soon after or about the same time as the Moore family—were two brothers, Braddock and Bartlett Varnum Weeks, and their first cousins Lafayette Chandler and George Washington Chandler. Their stories, and the stories of the two other Weeks brothers—Thomas Jefferson and Robinson Jones—form inter-locking pieces in Pescadero town's early history.

THOMAS JEFFERSON AND ROBINSON JONES WEEKS

In 1849 Thomas Jefferson Weeks, 18, and his married brother Robinson Jones Weeks, 29, steamed into San Francisco on board the *New Jersey*. Squeezed into dark fetid cabins, eating bad food and fighting off scurvy aboard what amounted to a floating tenement, it had taken them six months to sail 15,000 miles around Cape Horn.

On the ground young Thomas was off like a shot for the Gold Country. But prospecting proved to be such hard work, the society so rough, and the cost of living so high in the mining fields that he soon abandoned it and headed for Santa Cruz, where he heard Americans were prospering. There he discovered that farming potatoes, much in demand during the Gold Rush years, could earn him a fortune without so much of the grief. He raised some sheep, too, and later planted an extensive orchard that produced fruit at a profit. In time the level of his success could be seen in the magnificent house Thomas built for himself and his family. His home soon became the gathering place for other members of his family as they made their way to California.

Patriarch Thomas Weeks (top), born in 1788. (Above), *his son Thomas Jefferson Weeks' Santa Cruz residence in 1908. Located behind the present high school, the home still exists, converted to use as multiple housing.*

48 Portraits of Pescadero

The Weeks Family

I. Braddock Weeks (born 18th century) *m.* **Bethia Jones Weeks**
    II. Sophronio Weeks Chandler
    II. Lucy Weeks Chandler
        III. *Lafayette "Lafitte" or "Lafe" Chandler (b. 1833 Maine) *m.* Lizzie Garragus
            IV. Elma Chandler *m.* Asa Weeks (see below)
        III. *George Washington Chandler (10/13/1826 Maine – 5/13/1903 Santa Cruz) on 5/14/1861 *m.* **Martha Dounell**
            IV. Georgianna (b. 4/18/1862)
            IV. Lucy (b. 2/12/1866)
    II. THOMAS WEEKS (6/17/1788 Plymouth County, MA) *m.* **SARAH (SALLY) HARMON**
        III. BRADDOCK WEEKS (b. 1813 Maine – 7/07/1893 Pescadero) *m.* **CLARISSA** (b. 1818 Maine – 9/08/1887, Pescadero)
            IV. Albion (5/06/1843 Maine – 3/21/1908 Pescadero) *m.* **Margaret Hattabaugh**. No children.
            IV. Franklin (1847 Maine – 12/06/1872 Pescadero)
        III. Robinson Jones (R.J.) Weeks (b. 1820 Maine) *m.* **Cordelia Enfield Danforth** (7/01/1819 Maine – 9/23/1901 La Honda). Only two of their children are listed here:
            IV. Emily Danforth Weeks Knott (b. 1843 Maine)
            IV. Asa Thomas Weeks (3/01/1859 La Honda – 19? Pescadero) *m.* **Elma Chandler**
        III. THOMAS JEFFERSON WEEKS (b. 1831 Maine – ? Santa Cruz)
        III. BARTLETT VARNUM (B.V.) WEEKS (10/31/1832 Maine – 2/14/1910 Pescadero) *m.* **ANNIE JANE WASHBURN** ((8/23/1832 Maine – 1/28/1925 Pescadero)
            IV. George (?)
            IV. Twin Freddie (12/22/1867 Pescadero – 8/27/1871 Pescadero)
            IV. Twin **EDWARD WEEKS SR.** (12/22/1867 Pescadero – 1958 Pescadero) *m.* **HAZEL VIRGINIA BELL** (1885 San Francisco – 1972 Pescadero)
                V. Milton Weeks (1911 Pescadero)
                V. FRANCES (Fannie Louise) WEEKS (4/27/1916 Pescadero – 4/07/2003 Santa Cruz)
                V. Florence Virginia Weeks (7/15/1918 Pescadero – ?)
                V. Harold Weeks (8/22/1921 Pescadero – 5/13/2000)
                V. EDWARD WEEKS JR. (b. 1/24/1927 San Mateo)

*George and Lafayette Chandler were first cousins; we don't know which sister—Sophronio or Lucy—had which boy.

Above: *Braddock Weeks.* At right, *Robinson Jones Weeks and his wife, Cordelia, who founded the Weeks dynasty in La Honda.*

Meanwhile, since he came to California with the idea of acquiring land, not gold, brother R.J. Weeks stayed in San Francisco and ran a meat market on Stockton near Market Street to accumulate some capital. Men from all over the world stopped in San Francisco to get needed supplies and food, and to have some fun before launching off to the gold country. R.J. made good money in his business.

What a place! San Francisco had metastasized from the Spanish presidio, mission, and a scattering of ramshackle shanties in the sand dunes into a town of several substantial city buildings arranged around a public square. But banks, hotels, homes, and other public places had to be built and rebuilt many times. Between December of 1849 and the end of June 1851, the city was ravaged by six great fires and several smaller ones, costing more than $21 million in damages before a municipal fire department was organized. And as if mirroring an inherent instability in the affairs of men, earthquakes repeatedly shook citizens out of their sleep.

The Gold Rush—injecting massive amounts of cash, passion, and people crazed with the fever to acquire riches in a hurry—defined the character of San Francisco's burgeoning society. In a mostly masculine population of 30,000, daily events in San Francisco were fraught with murder, theft, arson, gambling, and general mayhem. Racism was rampant. And prices were astronomical—the exchange of goods and money escalated at a staggering pace. The people struggled to achieve a modicum of civilized behavior that was governed by law. In June 1851 the San Francisco Committee of Vigilance was formed and it set to work immediately to rectify the general disorder. But its enthusiasm was such

A hunting party. Braddock Weeks, with gun at far right, was a very patriotic gentleman. The boy at center—possibly his son, Frank—is dressed in an outfit that resembles a Union soldier's uniform. 1856 to early 1860s.

that spontaneous hangings and shootings were commonplace.

San Francisco was no place to raise a family. After his wife Cordelia Enfield Danforth and their 8-year-old daughter Emily arrived via the Isthmus of Panama in late November 1851, R.J. was ready to move on. He took his family and went down to Santa Cruz to join his brother Thomas.

There he got interested in another kind of mining and, taking advantage of the resources so abundant in that area, established a lime kiln business that was later owned by Henry Cowell. But the sparsely populated hinterlands of what was then still San Francisco County beckoned. After his son, Burt, was born on February 9, 1853, R.J. was finally able to fulfill his dream of acquiring land. He moved his family to a 1900-acre ranch in La Honda in 1854 and built a fine house.

Like all new California immigrants he made a living by adapting to circumstances. During his life R.J. made money as a farmer, a logger, and a hotel owner. This allowed him to keep close ties with family members who lived in a wide radius around him—from Santa Cruz to Searsville to Pescadero—even when he sojourned from time to time in other territories expanding his business. His son Asa Thomas Weeks (born March 1, 1859 in La Honda) was part of R.J.'s legacy to Pescadero, too. After a life of high adventure, 50-year-old Asa would migrate to Pescadero, marry Elma Chandler, and live out his days at the Level Lea Farm.

BRADDOCK [BRANAT] WEEKS

Born in 1813, Braddock was the eldest of the Weeks brothers. We know that he took the Isthmus of Panama route but it's not clear exactly

"My aunt, Mrs. Steele, told me that Bart Weeks was the bravest man she ever knew. He owned a lot of property near where the old high school was. Squatters would try to take over and throw lumber over the fence to build something. He would stand on the other side and throw it right back. The odds were against him as there were so many of them."

— Louise Moore Williamson, 1973

Bartlett Varnum Weeks and Annie Jane Washburn Weeks, married August 2, 1866 in San Francisco.

when he came to California and whether or not he traveled alone, with any of his brothers or with his own family. The facts available suggest a possible scenario. His wife, Clarissa, and his two sons, Albion and Frank, were all natives of Maine, the youngest born in 1847. One source says Braddock moved to Pescadero in 1852—an earlier date than that for Alexander Moore, but still one that resonates with the property deals going on at that time between Juan José Gonzàles and Eli Moore. Based on the *California Census of 1850*'s listing Thomas Weeks as a resident in Santa Cruz and Braddock in Pescadero, it's reasonable to assume that sometime between 1850 and 1852, Braddock was at least planning to settle here.

Braddock Weeks *was* the first Weeks to actually move to Pescadero to live. In 1856 he and Clarissa, 13-year-old Albion and 9-year-old Frank were raising their own golden potatoes on a 100-acre farm, looking over the fields to see whether or not their crop was growing faster than Alex Moore's.

Braddock and his wife also owned a part-interest with John Besse, Henry C. Bidwell—a veteran of the Mexican-American War—and Jon Rader in Pescadero's first mercantile store. Braddock would step out of the arrangement after two years, perhaps because the farmer in him was too much of an "outdoors" man. He was a firm supporter of other local civic institutions, too. He was one of the men who organized and paid for the early mail delivery service from Searsville, where his brother Bartlett lived, and later was one of the founders of the Congregational Church.

It's generally accepted that Braddock Weeks' house was built in 1860, but construction could have been started as early as 1856. The house still stands in almost the same spot across the creek from where his younger brother Bart lived, and today is one of the two oldest original pioneer homes built in Pescadero that still survive. Braddock lived in his house until he died on July 7, 1893; Clarissa had gone six years before him, following their youngest son Franklin who died at age 25 in 1872.

BARTLETT VARNUM WEEKS

Born in Kennebec County, Maine on October 31, 1832 Bartlett Varnum Weeks was 22 years old when he emigrated to California. He traveled by ship via Nicaragua and landed at San Francisco on January 28, 1854. After regaining his "land legs" by resting five or six months with Thomas in Santa Cruz, Bartlett Weeks relocated to Searsville where a *bona fide* town engaged in

Albion Weeks on the porch of his family home on Pescadero Creek Road, 1890s. Born in 1843, Albion was a bachelor most of his life; in his mid-fifties, he met and married a young Irish woman from San Francisco named Margaret Hattabaugh. Although quite a bit older than she, they both delighted in each other and their marriage was very happy. Albion died in 1908 at age 65. Margaret, still a very young woman, married John Dias Sr., a naturalized Azorean man working in the meat business in Pescadero, and together they raised a family of three children—John, Noel, and Margaret—in the old Braddock Weeks house.

lumbering had blossomed. Four years later he moved again, to join his older brother Braddock in Pescadero.

On May 20, 1858, Bartlett bought a chunk of the former Gonzàles land grant from Alexander Moore for the sum of $1,300 and started farming. He grew hay on 140 acres of hills he owned to the north of town now called Shade Ranch. Over the next few years, Bartlett had many more exchanges with Alexander Moore, not all of which were clear-cut. Santa Cruz records document a confusing flurry of land transactions between the two parties, sometimes describing the sale of the same parcel, or parts thereof, back and forth to each other. These troubles were due primarily to the indefinite boundaries outlined in the original Gonzàles land grant and "gave rise to unpleasantness" for a time but they were resolved eventually.

Two years later, in 1860, Bartlett acquired a 157-acre parcel from Juan Gonzàles's widow (Ana Rodrígues de Gonzàles) that included the Mexican adobe house, which she and her children probably vacated at this time. His farm is a historical spot, for it was here, years ago, that Gonzàles had erected an adobe dwelling, the first building of any kind constructed at Pescadero. The adobe, now long gone, stood where the original Spanish trail crossed Pescadero Creek. In 1866 Bartlett married Annie Jane Washburn, the sister of Sarah Swanton who was running the new hotel in Pescadero.

Bartlett and Annie Weeks had three children in all: a boy named George and twins Edward and Freddie. George is a mystery; there are no records of his birth or his life. The story goes that he was committed to a mental institution in Sonoma County even before his brothers were born; he then vanishes from the family's memory.

Edward Weeks Sr. and his twin brother Freddie were born in the Gonzàles adobe on December 22, 1867. The family lived there until 1872, a year after Freddie died. B.V. and Annie Weeks moved next door into an existing frame house that had been previously occupied. Later sources cite this house as being built by Bartlett in 1885; whether or not this is true, it is the same house on Goulson Street that is currently occupied by the third generation of the Weeks family.

Bartlett was an upstanding man in the community, just like Braddock. In 1867 he, too, helped to found the Congregational Church. As the years went by he helped to establish the Grange Bank and the Dairy Agency in San Francisco, as well as

Margaret Hattabaugh (Albion Weeks' widow) and second husband John Dias with their newborn son at the Crown 9 dairy, run by Manuel Dias. 1911–1913.

Timeline 1856 – 1879
Highlighted parallel events in San Francisco Bay Area, California, and the Nation

1860 Pony Express established. Letters cost $3 a half-pound and took 12 days to cross the continent from New York City to Sacramento.

By this year about one-fifth of California's population is composed of either domestic or immigrant Irish; by the 1870s, 30%.

1861 President Abraham Lincoln, a Republican (National Unionist), is inaugurated on March 4.

On April 12 the Civil War begins with the first bombardment of Fort Sumter.

The Emancipation Proclamation is first issued on September 22; and in November, Jefferson Davis is elected president of the Confederacy.

1863 The Emancipation Proclamation is enforced.

1864 Lincoln is re-elected on November 8.

1865 The Thirteenth Amendment formally outlaws slavery.

Five days after Lee surrenders to Grant at Appomattox, Lincoln is shot; he dies the next day on April 15. Vice President Andrew Jackson steps in.

On April 26 Johnston surrenders to Sherman.

On June 23, the Civil War is officially over when the last Confederate general, Stand Watie, surrenders.

1865 – 1868 Chinese—the first immigration of Asians to California—come to the Coast and take the lead in itinerant agricultural labor.

1866 Pescadero and Half Moon Bay Stage Co. is established by six coastside residents who buy a lot in Spanishtown, and by summer 1867 two stage companies are running twice daily between San Mateo and Pescadero.

1867 The Alaska Purchase.

1868 After seven years of petitioning by men such as John Garretson Pescadero becomes part of San Mateo County instead of Santa Cruz County.

1869 President Ulysses S. Grant, Republican, is inaugurated and serves two terms.

The transcontinental railroad is completed, opening up floods of new migrations to the West.

View looking west past Braddock Weeks' house, orchards and barns, gives a good idea of Pescadero town in the 1860–1870s.

1870s Racial distrust and hatred of Chinese grows into violence.

1872 Eve of nationwide financial panic and long depression.

1871 Indian Appropriation Act passes, making null and void any independent nation, tribe or power with whom the United States government would have to treat.

1875 On August 23-27 Ralston's Bank of California fails.

1877 President Rutherford B. Hayes, a Republican, is inaugurated and serves one term.

1879 Thomas Edison invents the light bulb.

the Farmers Mutual Fire Insurance Company, one of the first of its kind to offer such protection to farmers. On July 15, 1873, when the California State Grange came into being, Bartlett took on the responsibility of representing Pescadero. The Grange was a forward-thinking organization from its inception—38 years before California passed women's suffrage, the Grange accepted women as equal members. Some familiar Pescadero names that appear on its early registers include the Aldred Woodhams; B.V. Weeks; Mrs. Eli Daniel Moore; the Spragues; and I.C. Steele.

Lafayette "Lafitte" Chandler

Lafayette Chandler (named after the Marquis de Lafayette) left home when he was 20, bound for San Francisco via Nicaragua on the steamship *S.S. Lewis*. Coming into the Golden Gate on an April day in 1853 under heavy fog, the ship foundered on a reef of rocks as it approached the shore, but all passengers were safely landed. Lafayette shook off this near misadventure and picked up a steamer headed for Santa Cruz to rendezvous with his cousin, Thomas Weeks.

The two young men had many things to discuss, not the least of which was where Lafayette should ultimately live. In the fall Lafayette rode up to Pescadero to look around. He stayed a couple of months, then returned to Santa Cruz before going up to Searsville in San Mateo County to check in with cousin Bart.

Asa Weeks (top), the son of Robinson Jones Weeks and Cordelia Danforth Weeks, was born in La Honda on March 1, 1859. A graduate of St. Matthew's Military Academy in San Mateo, he spent many years farming, mining and running sawmills in La Honda, Idaho, Montana, British Columbia, Alaska, and Mexico. When he was 50 years old he came back to San Francisco and in 1909 married Elma Chandler (above) the only child of Lafitte Chandler and Lizzie Garragus. In 1910 Asa and Elma moved into the old Lafe Chandler place at Level Lea Farm in Pescadero and farmed and raised stock on 200 acres there until the end of Asa's life.

Nothing else seemed so fine to him as Pescadero. In 1854 Lafayette went into partnership running a dairy ranch with his older cousin George Washington Chandler. He lived in a little farmhouse just south of Pescadero Road. Three years later Lafitte and George went in together on a 171-acre farm called "Level Lea." They kept about 60 head of cows, manufacturing butter and cheese. This was Lafitte's permanent home ever since, with time out for one visit home to the Eastern states in 1867 and occasional stints later on working in Washington and Idaho with his cousin R.J. Weeks.

George Chandler was 26 when he and Lafitte set sail for California. While they were farming at Level Lea, he went back to Maine in 1860 to visit family and to court his sweetheart, Martha Dounell. On May 14, 1861 they married and returned to Pescadero. The newlyweds soon had two children: Georgiana, born April 18, 1862, and Lucy, born February 12, 1866.

In July 1866, George left Level Lea to work as a lumberman at New Year's Canyon. Lumber suited George better than dairying or farming and he stuck with it. By early 1867 George, in partnership with J.C. Hawley and George Harrington, started construction of the Glen Mill, later known as the Chandler and Harrington Mill. The mill ran until at least 1877 and was sold four years later to an Oakland buyer. Chandler and Harrington both left White House Canyon. George Chandler went up to Humboldt County to work timber and never moved back to Pescadero.

Lafitte bought out his cousin George's share of Level Lea in 1869 and in the early '70s married his first wife, Lizzie Garragus. According to one of Lafitte's descendants, Meredith Reynolds, "They built a two-story Victorian house on the north side of the road where the bunkhouse stands now. [Their daughter] Elma was born in 1874. Her mother died just 18 months later from a boil on her chin." Lizzie Garragus Chandler was 24 years old. After a period of mourning Lafitte married again. His second wife was named Margaret ("Maggie") Stokes.

"My father, Lafe Chandler, was feeble, and on November 1st, 1910, we rented the farm for $1,000 a year. From the first we had trouble with my stepmother, but she has ever been a small woman in the life-plan."

— Elma Chandler Weeks, 1927.

Top: *Lafe Chandler and workers show off 1,270 sacks of barley from their harvest. 1908.*
Inset left: *Margaret and Lafe Chandler. 1908 – 1911.*
Above: *Elma Chandler grooms her dogs.*
Left: *Asa Weeks in his field of 8-foot high Windsor beans. July 1920.*
Opposite page, inset: *Lafe Chandler's Victorian house at Level Lea Farm.*

All photos this page: Meredith Reynolds Collection.

The Weeks Family 57

The House on Goulson Street

EDWARD WEEKS, SR.

Edward, born on December 22, 1867 in the old adobe house, grew up as an only child. His twin, Freddie, died before reaching the age of four of either diptheria or scarlet fever and was buried in the Pescadero cemetery, which at that time belonged to the Weeks family. There was another boy, George, but we don't know when he was born. Frances Weeks says that her father never knew much about George and never talked about him as this brother had been placed in a mental institution in Sonoma County while very young. After his father Bartlett died, Edward continued paying for George's support for many years until a relative who lived in San Jose—an attorney possessing a larger income—offered to take over the bills. The family never learned when George died.

Edward went to Pescadero's elementary school until he was 12. Then his parents sent him to board and study at St. Matthew's Military School in San Mateo, like his cousin Asa Weeks. After graduating Edward worked for a while as a fine carpenter; Ed Weeks says that in this work, his father was a true artist. Edward also went into dairying and started some creameries making cheese. One of these creameries is still standing at Lafayette Chandler's Level Lea Farm on Pescadero Road.

Ed Weeks recalls that his father was "kind of eccentric—he was always inventing things." As he never cared much for farming, Edward's active mind drove him to wander from one new venture to another. He traveled around for several years, setting up another creamery at Willetts among other things. His life took an abrupt turn when his father, Bartlett Varnum Weeks, died on Valentine's Day, 1910. Edward was working as a carpenter in San Francisco at the time and returned to look after his mother and the family farm in Pescadero. Edward—at 45 an apparently confirmed bachelor—was soon to be transformed into a husband and householder.

Built in 1885 by B.V. Weeks, the family home, seen ca. 1915.

In 1863 Charles Swanton, a 40-year-old blacksmith from Maine, opened an entertainment establishment called the Swanton House in a hotel that had been previously built and run by Samuel Bean and then Loren Coburn. His wife, Sarah Washburn—Annie Washburn Weeks's 29-year-old sister—ran the hotel business, catering to sportsmen and holiday-makers who came in to town to enjoy the scenery. They employed two Chinese cooks; a house servant and a chamber maid. Their son, Franklin (born 1853 in Maine), lived in the hotel, as did Peter G. Stryker, a retail merchant from New York, and Daniel Wilson, a grocer from Canada.

"My great-grandfather [Plummer]...my mother, and grandmother [Bell] must have come down to stay at the Swanton House and that's where my parents met. He [Edward Weeks] was so much older, my grandmother didn't like the idea—Grandma [Bell] was always very fussy and stand-offish, she was a social climber, I think—and my Grandpa Bell did not like it either. He didn't like my dad much. But that was how they got together."

— Frances Weeks Dubel, 2003

Edward Weeks met his future wife—a lovely, accomplished young lady 18 years younger than himself named Hazel Virginia Bell—at the Swanton House run by his aunt, Sarah Washburn Swanton. The Swanton House had been in business for nearly 50 years in 1910 and had expanded over the decades to include a complement of cottages to attract a sophisticated clientele from San Francisco. When they weren't on holiday at their summerhouse in Inverness, the Bells, and their in-laws the Plummers, might have

The Weeks Family 59

come down the Coast with some regularity to escape the heat and noise of the City.

Like Edward, Hazel, too, was an only child, the daughter of Dr. Henry Bell, a physician in San Francisco, and his wife, Fannie Plummer. Hazel came from a privileged background. She had been to finishing school in the East and had come away with an interest in drama that sparked her imagination her whole life. Perhaps she might have invented many scenes that could be played out in her family's home. It was filled with beautifully handcrafted furnishings, some of which had been made by her Grandfather Plummer, who was an accomplished woodworker. From fine bookcases to a sewing cupboard with tiny drawers, Grandpa Plummer was your man. Hazel's mother was fond of reminding her that Grandpa Plummer had made all the cabinetry for the Pullman train cars!

The Bells and their San Francisco house had survived the great 1906 earthquake with stories to tell of it. Fannie Bell's great-granddaughter, Ruth Dubel Ditty, recalls this one:

"My great-Grandmother did talk about the earthquake [San Francisco, 1906] when my great-grandfather was a doctor up there. She talked about the break in the gas line on Market Street or wherever it was, and Great-Grandpa Bell would have to ride the buggy down so far, then cross over and get into another buggy to go someplace else. She talked about the people they took—some of them went out to an island to get away from the fire, was it Angel Island? She said that people there were dragging empty trunks. They'd drag them for blocks. She saw a lady carrying a birdcage with the bird in it. That's all—she had her nightgown and the birdcage and the bird. People were just in a state of shock. I remember her talking about the office building, seeing it sway back and forth."

Edward Weeks, of Pescadero, was not intimidated by the Bells' cosmopolitan lifestyle. He was a very intelligent and handsome man with a lot of

experience of his own. His charm must have matched his looks—Ed Weeks says that he didn't know how successful his father was or how much of a businessman, but he was always a fairly healthy and good-sized man. Having inherited a house and a livelihood, Edward had a strong incentive to marry and he was strongly attracted to this young beauty. He made up his mind that it was Hazel Bell that he wanted to be his companion in this new phase of his life.

Against her parents' misgivings about the difference in their ages, Hazel opted in favor of her strong attraction to Edward. After all, her own mother was 17 years younger than her father—a Southern gentleman from Virginia—and he'd always treated her mother "like a China doll!" The courtship between Edward and Hazel was incandescent; they were married within the year on October 9. After honeymooning at the Ahwanee Hotel in fashionable Yosemite they set up housekeeping in the Weeks family home in Pescadero.

Perhaps Edward and Hazel's marriage was too precipitous for both sets of in-laws. Annie Weeks moved out of the Weeks family home and into a little house next door that Edward built for her. Frances remembers that her grandmother Annie Weeks and her mother didn't get along well.

"My grandmother [Annie Weeks]…called my mother 'devilish jade' and to her that was pretty bad. I used to go over there. I remember her ginger snap cookies. I loved them. My mother never could make them to suit me. I think there was a little bit of jealousy there because I spent a lot of time with my grandmother."

In spite of her resolve to follow her heart, and having acted upon it, life in Pescadero was strikingly different for Hazel as well as it *(Continued on page 64)*

Opposite page: *Edward Weeks in one of his dairy creameries;* (above) *a detail of its immaculate machinery.*
Inset: *Edward—always willing to try new things—and his bicycle.*
Right: *Edward, 42. March 6, 1910. In these and in all photographs taken of him during his life, Edward's posture and disciplined bearing reflect his strength of character.*

The Weeks Family

Left: *Hazel and 8-month-old Milton, the first-born. 1911.*
Above: *Milton with great-Grandpa Plummer. 1911.*
Right: *Toddler Frances "Fannie" Weeks. 1917.*

The Weeks' Kids' Family Album

Left: *Fannie and Florence playing in their yard, about 1918.*

Above: *Milton (11); Harold (1); Florence (4); Fannie (6) in 1922.*
Left: *Family roses, about 1911.*

62   Portraits of Pescadero

Top left and center: *The first two Weeks' kids, Milton and Fannie, were good friends from the start.*
Below: *Florence and Fannie play next door at Grandma Annie Weeks' house.*

Below left and center: *Fannie with the last Weeks' baby, Edward Washburn Weeks. Ed was Fannie's "living doll" and much-loved companion, sometimes accompanying her to school when no one else at home could watch him.*
Right: *From left, Milton, Fannie, neighbor Walter Moore and Ed Jr. on the porch at home. 1932.*

The Weeks Family 63

(Continued from page 61) was for Edward. Raised in a sophisticated city environment, tempered by Southern gentility, Hazel had social aspirations. She'd been accustomed to living in a household in which functions were performed by invisible hands, managed by her mother and paid for by her father. In Pescadero there was no hired help in the kitchen. There was no electricity, no gas, and no maid service, as there were in her San Francisco home. Suddenly she was no longer a protected young lady with a carefree disposition but a 25-year-old woman with her own household to run and pregnant with the first of her five children.

Milton was born at home a year later on August 12, 1911, probably attended by Pescadero's own Dr. Thompson. Louise Williamson, Hazel's closest friend, was there with her when Fannie Bell (Frances), the second child, arrived on April 27, 1916. Milton called her "Red Root" because of her vibrant color at birth.

Frances later said that the kids were all born about five years apart except for her sister, Florence, who "was thrown in extra" two years after Frances on July 15, 1918. Despite their closeness in age the two girls didn't have much in common; "Florence always ran around with kids younger, and I always went with kids older." Frances remembered—without bitterness—that her father always called her the "Smart One" and her sister, the "Pretty One."

The second boy, Harold, was born August 22, 1921 "in San Mateo at a friend's house, who was a midwife. She worked with Grandpa Bell when he had his practice in San Francisco. [My mother] went over and stayed with [her] when she had the baby."

The last child, Edward Washburn Weeks—the Ed Weeks who still lives on Goulson Street—was born at Mills Memorial Hospital on January 24, 1927 when Frances was about 10 years old. Frances remembers that "My mother developed an infection in her finger, I think they called it a [felon]. ... She couldn't put her hands in water. I was the only one old enough and big enough to take care of the baby, so Edward was my 'living doll'—I bathed him and took care of him, so I've always felt a little bit closer to him than to the rest of them."

THE FAMILY ORCHESTRA

Both Frances and Ed Jr. say that their father's biggest interest in life was music. Edward Sr. made sure each of his children learned to play an instrument as soon as their small hands could hold one, whether they wanted to or not. And the children played

Dr. Henry and Mrs. Fannie Plummer Bell with their daughter Hazel in 1891; the Bells' home in San Francisco; 18-year-old Hazel Virginia Bell in 1903.

Left to right: Frances (Fannie); Edward Sr.; Milton, wearing glasses; Harold; Hazel; and Florence. 1924.

---

whatever instrument Edward chose for them. The family practiced at home together regularly. It was always classical music. From inside the Weeks' house passing townspeople might hear over the creek's gentle murmur the sounds of a violin, piano, xylophone, cello, flute, coronet, or a clarinet.

Edward's dream was for the whole family to perform together as a small concert orchestra, perhaps even to get a job playing dinner music on an ocean liner. The violin was his instrument; and Hazel played piano in spite of being partially deaf, an affliction she attributed to her father having brought home diptheria one time after treating patients when she was a girl. Milton played clarinet. Frances's mother started her on piano, but as soon as she took up the 3/4-sized cello she wasn't allowed to touch the piano again except to tune her own instrument. Florence learned to play the flute and Harold, at age 3, "a little bitty" violin. They performed at evening events and in churches. One time they went to San Francisco and played in a program that was broadcast over the radio. The full extent of Edward's idea was never realized, but the Weeks family was nevertheless admired in Pescadero for their talents and abilities. Everyone always said they were all very smart kids.

Frances was her father's favorite and the only one of the Weeks' kids to receive formal music training. One year her father took her down in the car to Santa Cruz for weekly music lessons. When she'd learned everything she could from her teacher, he took her up to San Francisco for another year-and-a-half to study with the director of a symphony orchestra that played in one of the big hotels. Frances loved going to the musician's beautiful apartment on Russian Hill with its view of the whole bay and staying overnight at her grandparents' house. It was an all-day trek to go from

The Weeks Family Orchestra

Left: *Young bride Hazel Bell Weeks at the piano in her Pescadero living room. 1910.*

Far right, top: *Milton shows the youngest Weeks how to handle the clarinet with good form.* Center: *Harold gets the hang of the baby violin.* Bottom: *Florence, on flute, and Fannie, with her 3/4-sized cello, are ready to perform.*

Right: *Ed Weeks Jr. practices the clarinet but not for too long, as he is the last in the line of family musicians to take the stage and the orchestra is already disbanding.*

66 *Portraits of Pescadero*

The Weeks Family Orchestra at home: Frances (Fannie), age 12, on cello; Edward Sr., 60, on violin; Harold, 7, on violin; Hazel, 43, on piano; Florence, 10, on flute; and Milton, 17, on clarinet. 1928.

Pescadero to San Francisco. And travel was sometimes an adventure, too. If an ocean fog was too thick, someone would have to get out of the car and walk holding a light in front of it so the driver could see the road.

When the family "orchestra" practice was over each day, Frances would have to practice with her parents as part of a "trio." This extra practice seemed like punishment after a while. Frances was expected, like all her siblings, to get top grades—"You know, I was a Weeks, I wasn't allowed to do anything that wasn't top-notch"—but her priority was always to practice her music before doing her school homework. Her father set a strict daily schedule for her to practice an hour in the morning before she went to school and an hour when she got home. She invented various strategies to get out of it. At one point she "got real good at setting the clock ahead an hour" while her father was out in the barn milking the cow so she could skip practice and go right to her studies. Much of her girlhood life was centered on reading everything she could lay hands on. Besides her studies she devoured travel books, historical novels, anything that opened up a wider world to her curious mind. Frances was an excellent student and became Salutatorian of her high school class.

An Independent Mind

The Weeks were known as a very respectable and responsible family. Edward was a member of Pescadero Lodge, No. 226, I.O.O.F.; he and Hazel both belonged to the Daughters of Rebekah. But as a father, Edward Weeks was an immovable force, strict and stern, and sometimes given to "quite a temper."

"I remember one time he lined us all up in the kitchen on that step thing in the dining room area and got out the shotgun. I thought he was going to blow us all to hell, I guess. My mother says, 'You can't scare me with that gun, it's not even loaded!' He said, 'By God, I'll show you,' and he put a shotgun shell in it. By that time Milton had sneaked out and gone next door to the neighbor's and they came over and put a stop to things. That was the only time I really saw him almost out of his mind. I don't know what caused it. What a temper he had.

"He kept liquor in the house because he liked it for medication purposes. He'd have a hot toddy once in a while, when he had a cold or something like that. And smoke—he called cigarettes 'pimp sticks.' Once in a while he'd buy a pack of cigarettes and he'd smoke one or two and then throw it away, burn it too."

Her father's volatile disposition made Frances wary. She was not allowed to date: she could not even go with her brothers to the school dances; only her mother would do. Nor could she see the movies on Friday nights because she had to get up early the next morning to go to her cello lesson in San Francisco.

But Frances had a high spirit and a rebellious streak, too. Friends she made in high school were friends for life—Elaine Shaw and Dorothy Nunes, Elizabeth Morimoto. Frances in later years told her daughter, Ruth, that sometimes they "used to go down to Bean Hollow for the picnics." Several of her friends had cars and four or five of them would get together at one of the school basketball games and sneak off for a ride. Frances admitted that there might be a little necking along the way, but nothing serious. The kids would always get back just in time to avoid trouble—"You had to be careful what you did because you knew darn well it was gonna get back to your dad some way or another anyway."

Frances ran away from home when she was 17. When she graduated from high school in 1932 her Bell grandparents had

Top: *A free-spirited young woman with a mind of her own, Frances launches herself into the Great Depression. 1933.*
Center: *That's Frances in center front of her 1932 high school class. 1928.*
Bottom: *Now educated in a trade that could earn her an income, Frances looks polished and confident. 1934 or '35.*

offered to send her to study at the San Francisco Conservatory of Music but her father said no, Frances was too young to leave home. She went back to high school for another year as a post-graduate and took classes in algebra and Spanish. She'd somehow managed to keep up with the piano on the sly and played it for the operetta the school put on every year. As a way of honoring her contribution, the school invited her to attend their annual junior-senior banquet in San Francisco. Again her father said no. Frances thought, "By God, I'm gonna go anyhow."

In the meantime she'd been working as a "mother's aide" and housekeeper on one of the local ranches. Since there was nothing to spend money on in Pescadero she saved everything she'd made. Then she heard that some of her friends were going up to take entrance exams at the University

of California and she wanted to do that too. She told her mother she was going to leave and that a Japanese boy—a friend from school—would be picking her up the next morning. Hazel promised not to say anything to her husband and she kept her word. The kids came by to pick Frances up while it was still dark and before the sun rose she was gone.

It was 1933 and although the Depression was damping the nation's spirit like a load of mildewed laundry, 17-year-old Frances paid it no mind. She contacted her brother, Milton, who was going to school at Berkeley. Through him she managed to get a room in the same boarding house; immediately she applied to a nearby secretarial school and got a job as a mother's helper to support herself while she went to school. Within a few days, however, her grandparents in San Francisco insisted that she talk

Edward Weeks Sr., on his Cleveland tractor, works the fields. Above, Giannini's barn. 1918.

Top: *Milton, Frances, and Florence, like all the other kids growing up in Pescadero, spent hours playing in the creek.*
Above: *The four oldest Weeks' kids also had many adventures at Lake Lucerne—where Ed later nearly drowned one time—and at the nearby beaches.*

it over with them before doing something rash. Grandpa Bell didn't approve of the secretarial school idea. He said, "Being a secretary was about as much good as being a nurse in reputation." And he would know, being a doctor and all.

Milton escorted Frances to their grandparents' house in San Francisco and very shortly thereafter her father came up from Pescadero to give her a piece of his mind. The first thing he said was, "You're going to get a free ride home, young lady!" But her grandparents stuck adamantly to the notion that she go on with her education and said, "She is not!" Edward was forced to go back home without her.

Frances never did return to Pescadero to live, although many years later, after she'd married and had her own daughter, she thought about buying a house in her childhood home.

"I always liked Pescadero because it was kind of a quiet, easy-going place. There wasn't a lot of crime, I don't think anybody ever got killed or shot outside of some old, ancient history. It was just a nice little town. I knew practically everybody there."

EDWARD WASHBURN WEEKS

When Frances left home Ed was only seven years old and the baby of the family. Florence and Harold were still at home but were so much older than Ed they led their own lives and would soon be gone. Too young to play an instrument in the family orchestra, Ed missed out on the years of heavy discipline exacted by his father. Ed's childhood memories reflect a wonderful time when boys could have great fun doing simple things and playing with "toys" conceived of their own invention.

One of Ed's close friends was Tim Grigsby, who lived on the corner of Goulson and North streets. The boys made bean blowers that they cut out of the tubular stems of wild parsley that grew across the road. They tied "loads of timber" onto small wagons; rode tricycles and walked around on stilts; played hide-and-go-seek and kick-the-can. And the creek offered endless possibilities. Ed learned to swim in a spot across the street from where his house stands today when he was about 10 years old, and caught his first fish 200 feet from his porch.

As a boy, Ed had responsibilities, too. *"One thing I had to do was milk the cow when I got a little older. We had a cow down by the barn and I would take her up to the cemetery before school. After school I would go up and get her, bring her home, milk her and take her to the barn. I don't care much for milking. I always felt sorry for people who had to milk more than one cow. One was all I could stand."*

Ed made pocket money delivering the *Cal Bulletin* to about 30 customers for a penny a paper. His earnings for a month would amount to 90 cents, enough to buy some candy. The kids would take the stash and go up in the barn, stack up the hay, and eat sweets until their stomachs groaned.

During the Depression years Ed's Dad was in his late sixties and could no longer work artichokes in the fields in back of the house. He rented his land to the Kuwahara family and they raised lettuce of such beautiful quality it was highly praised about town. Everyone in the family had to be equally inventive. Ed says,

"I remember back during the Depression, my mother used to feed the younger school children from the elementary school during lunch time. We had picnic tables out in the middle of the walnut trees. We would get government food—I really didn't know where it came from at that time. We would get oranges."

In 1939 the Weeks family took over their land again. Ed's sister's family (Florence and Albert Pomi) raised beans, broccoli, beets, carrots, cauliflower, and cabbage for about five years, all managed from afar by brother Milton who had a civilian job working for the Navy in Alameda. The land was mortgaged during the Depression years, so after the War when Ed was about 18 the family decided to sell it. Their current neighbor Joe Giannini bought it and lived in the Weeks house for 10 years, raising artichokes—Ed says he was one of the best farmers. Ed Weeks bought it back in 1955, for $4,500, and has lived in his family house on Goulson Street ever since.

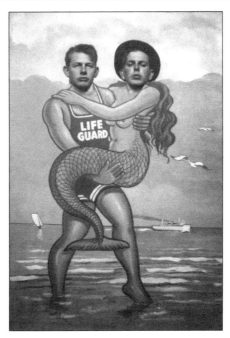

Far left: *Ed Weeks' high school graduation photo, 1940.*

Near left: *Ed remembers that he and his good friend Evatt Vierra enjoyed this day at the Santa Cruz wharf in the best of good spirits. 1945.*

Meredith Reynolds Collection.

The Kuwahara brothers rented most of Asa and Elma Weeks' farmland on share in 1918; later, in the '30s, they also grew beautiful lettuces on Edward Weeks' property in back of the house on Goulson Street.

Interview with Walter Hohl, June 24, 2003. Pescadero Historical Society.

Personal interviews with *Pam McReynolds* (7/07/2003); *Meredith Reynolds*; and *Ed Weeks*. Pescadero Historical Society.

Lyon, Mary Louise — "A Portion of the History of the Patrons of Husbandry in San Mateo County 1860 – 1900." 1800 SM: student monograph in San Mateo County Historical Museum Archives.

Sources

All photographs are from the Frances Weeks Dubel and Edward Washburn Weeks Collections archived in the Pescadero Historical Society inventory unless otherwise noted.

Alexander, Philip W. — *History of San Mateo County*. Burlingame Publishing Co., CA 1916.

Alley, B.F. — *History of San Mateo Co.* 1883.

Blount, Clinton — *A Conversation with Ed Weeks*. Albion Environmental, Inc. November 7, 2002.

Census and *voter registries* for Santa Cruz County and San Mateo County, various years.

Edmonds, John G. — *Union Cemetery, Redwood City, California*; Historic Union Cemetery Association. 2000, 2001)

Interview with Ruth Dubel Ditty, Feb. 21, 2004. Pescadero Historical Society.

Interview with Frances Weeks Dubel, Mar. 29, 2003. Pescadero Historical Society.

The Bartlett V. Weeks' house on Goularte Street. 97-350 Documents in San Mateo County Historical Museum Archives.

McCloud, Roy Walter — *History of San Mateo County, California* (Vol. II); Chicago, IL, The S.J. Clarke Publishing Co. 1928.

Mount Hope Cemetery list

Online: *History of Maine.* maine.gov/
Also, history of Searsville; San Mateo County; Santa Cruz County.

Pearl, Colleen — *Oral History on Thelma Keys*. Independent study. 1984. Loaned by Meredith Reynolds.

Stoltz, Nancy Elizabeth — *History of the Weeks Ranch at La Honda*. Midpeninsula Regional Open Space District monograph; Woodside, CA 2002.

Weeks, Asa — *Along the Life Trail, A sketch of the life and adventures of Asa Thomas Weeks*. (Manuscript donated by Meredith Reynolds.)

The Shaw Family
Elaine Baldwin Shaw

Elaine Shaw (Steele) at an annual Pescadero high school reunion in Memorial Park. August 18, 1999.

Elaine Shaw, daughter of John Elias Shaw Sr. and Ruth Baldwin Shaw, was born on October 10, 1916 on the Shaw Ranch, a second-generation member of the Shaw and Goulson families that were native to Pescadero. When she was very young her mother died in childbirth leaving her father to raise Elaine and her siblings. Elaine's family life in her girlhood was marked by this loss, but the Shaws transformed their sadness into a closeness that might be considered rare under any circumstances.

Elaine's father, like his father, was a farmer. Elaine grew up on the land her grandparents, Elias and Maria Shaw, bought in the 1870s. She learned early on how to get along best in life by helping out in whatever ways she could, to appreciate what she had and to let everything else go. She loved to be outdoors. The family kept animals for food and work—chickens, pigs, dairy cows, horses—and also had several compliments of pets through the years. Dogs and cats are often featured in family photographs. Although there was always lots of work, simple pleasures abounded for the Shaw kids: creek-walking; picnicking at the beach; picking and sampling berries in the hot summer sun until their fingers and tongues were stained purple from the fruit.

Elaine graduated from Pescadero Union High School in 1933, a year after her father died. In 1936 she married Stanley Steele, a man from a well-established Coast family that had longtime connections with the Pescadero community and the Shaw family. The Steeles' life was familiar—they were farmers, too—and Elaine made the transition gracefully. She moved to Stanley's home at Chalk Ridge Orchard and into another close family circle. As the years went by, she had two babies; Stanley's parents died; her girls got married and had their own kids. Sometime after Stanley died in 1990 she moved to Scotts Valley, where she lives today.

Elaine Steele will be 90 this year. Her stories are down-to-earth and often very funny, giving us insights into what life was like for many people in Pescadero long ago. In this way, she invites us into her own family and we come to know who they were and who she is, real people like you and me.

The Pioneer Generation

JOHN GOULSON

John Goulson was born April 12, 1815 in Lincolnshire, England on the Duke of Rutland's estate. Rebuilt in 1816 after a terrible fire nearly destroyed it, Belvoir Castle sat grandly on a hill overlooking the Vale of Belvoir (pronounced "Beaver"), where a long-since vanished Norman manor once stood. Goulson was a blacksmith. He practiced a trade that had been handed down in the Goulson line from father to son for many generations at Belvoir. He was married and had a child, Maria, born May 27, 1840; his house and livelihood were settled for life. But when he was 33, he broke with this 200-year-old tradition in a bold decision to leave England.

Profound changes were taking place in his homeland. The Industrial Revolution had swept over Britain and Europe since the eighteenth century, initiating a period of great social upheaval. Increasing mechanization and technological advances replaced cottage industry and, as traditional occupations disappeared and the demand for new skills grew, laborers moved off the land and into the cities.

When John Goulson was born the working force was growing in political power by forming guilds and trade unions. Then in 1839, shortly after the young Victoria was crowned, a movement demanding electoral reform and universal male suffrage arose. By 1846 it had developed into a crisis. On May 16, 1846 the Corn [Grain] Laws were repealed in spite of heated resistance against the repeal by powerful members of the Conservative Party and by the landed gentry.

The Corn Laws had imposed tariffs that were intended to protect English farmers from having to compete with cheap foreign grain imports, but the market reality was quite different. The threat really came not from abroad but from cheaper products made inside the country or imported from other British companies that dotted the Empire's map. The "farmers" most affected were not from the multitudes of poor people, but were the wealthy landowners. The age of feudalism was on its way out; free trade threatened not only the income generated by the great estates, but the political power historically associated with the upper class.

This portrait of Maria Goulson and Elias Shaw commemorates their marriage in San Francisco on October 10, 1866. The couple moved shortly after to Pescadero and began farming and raising babies.

The Shaw Family

I. ELIAS SHAW [2/03/1828 – 9/11/1894] *m.* **MARIA GOULSON** [5/27/1840 – 5/16/1919]

    II. Annie Shaw [1867 – 1928] *m.* Dan Adair [1865 – 1933]. Kids: Bertha; Miriam; Maria; Henry.

    II. Edgar Shaw [1869 – 1935]. Never married.

    II. Bertha Shaw [8/13/1872 – 1953] *m.* Ben Blaisdell. No children.

    II. Grace Shaw [10/05/1875 – 5/14/1956] *m.* Frank George [b. 7/04/1884]. No children.

    II. JOHN ELIAS SHAW SR. [10/05/1877 – 2/14/1932]

        m. **RUTH BALDWIN** [11/09/1882 – 4/12/1919]

        III. John Elias Shaw Jr. [12/21/1911 – 1/10/1999]

        III. Carol Gertrude Shaw [11/25/1912 – 10/31/1979]

        III. Ruth Mary Shaw [b. 3/10/1914]

        III. ELAINE BALDWIN SHAW [b. 10/10/1916] *m.* **STANLEY STEELE** [11/18/1907 – 7/11/1990]

            IV. RUTH LOUISE STEELE [b. 4/08/1938] *m.* **CLIFFORD JAMES MOORE** [b. 5/15/1933]

            IV. Sandra Jean Steele [b. 10/21/1940]

    II. Charles Evans and James Goulson Shaw [7/28/1882 – (James) 1935]

These events directly affected the lives of the Goulsons. In 1848, the year Goulson made his unprecedented decision to leave, 68-year-old John Henry Manners, the fifth Duke of Rutland, held tenure at Belvoir. He was probably not very active politically, but his son Charles, the Marquess of Granby, was. As a prominent politician in the Conservative Party, Granby had fought strenuously against the Corn Laws' repeal. He became the Party's leader in the British House of Commons at the beginning of 1848, and within months teamed up with Benjamin Disraeli and John Charles Herries. Granby—who would be the next Duke of Rutland—was clearly on the opposite side of the common man.

The old settled way of life on the Duke's estate, with its rigid definitions of social "place," low expectations for advancement and diminishing security, was no longer working. In 1848 the Goulson family—John, his wife, Sarah, and his 8-year-old daughter Maria—left England for the United States. The five-week voyage was rough sailing across the Atlantic on a creaky old vessel named the *Franconia*. It was lucky for the Goulsons they made it, for on the following trip across the ocean the *Franconia* sank.

Safely arrived in New York, the Goulsons struck out immediately for Wisconsin, where hundreds of other English folks were immigrating at the time. They settled in an English-sounding place

John Goulson, near right, and Elias Shaw, far right. Despite a significant difference in their ages, these two men forged deep bonds of friendship and trust through their common experiences, and, by marriage, became two of the founding pioneers of early Pescadero.

called Avon, and John set up his smithy. Wisconsin, newly admitted as the Union's 30th state, was growing rapidly. Lumber and wheat fed the economy and both industries provided ample opportunities to make a good living for a master mechanic such as Goulson.

Four years passed before the lure of a more temperate climate and better prospects in the West caught up with John Goulson. California had become a state in 1850 and was wide open to American settlement. In the spring of 1852, the family started for the gold fields in an ox team-drawn wagon, part of the same group of hopeful pioneers as a young Ohio farmer named Elias Shaw.

Elias Shaw

Elias Shaw was born on February 3, 1828 into a Pennsylvania Dutch family that lived in Meigs County, Ohio, near the Ohio River. Elias, his father and brothers were farmers; each year they built a raft of hardwood logs, loaded it with the produce they'd raised, and floated down the Ohio River to its junction with the Mississippi, then on down the Mississippi to the New Orleans market. When their produce was sold, they broke up the raft and sold the timber, too, before returning home by steamboat.

In 1848 a man named James Marshall found a pea-sized nugget of gold in the stream behind his boss's gristmill in the far-off territory of Mexican California. This discovery couldn't be kept a secret, no matter how hard Marshall's boss, John Sutter, tried to keep it quiet. Within weeks it seemed like everyone in the world knew about it.

Beginning in the 1830s, first-hand accounts written by the earliest white American explorers and mountain men to see California had been circulating broadly on the East Coast. The news of Marshall's discovery, spreading first by word of mouth and then by newspaper and magazine articles, initiated a great hysteria all over "civilized" America. Literally thousands of people dropped everything and bee-lined, by land or sea, for Sutter's Mill and its surrounding territory.

By 1852 the whole country east of Missouri was inflamed by the stories of the fabulous gold fields, and the fever wouldn't cool. Like everyone else who hadn't already left, Elias watched as the

Annie Shaw   Grace Shaw   Bertha Shaw   John Elias Shaw

Elias Shaw   Charles Shaw   Maria Shaw   James Shaw   Edgar Shaw

Above: *The Shaw family portrait was taken July 17, 1892 by Asher C. Maxcy in Pescadero.*
Below: *The Shaw Ranch.*

The Shaw Family   77

biggest mass migration in history rolled Westward in canvas-covered wagons. In those days, having a job usually meant working on the farm and opportunities for another kind of life were few. Elias was 24 years old and determined to expand his chances. In the spring he joined one of the hundreds of wagon trains departing from St. Joseph, Missouri. As luck would have it, he met an English blacksmith named John Goulson, his wife, and 12-year-old daughter, Maria, among his fellow travelers.

In the months that followed, Goulson and Shaw became friends, bonded by the intense experiences they shared despite the 13-year difference in their ages. The overland trip across the Plains was grueling, a long, tedious journey filled with daily hardships. Like many others who made this great journey, the Goulsons lost a child along the way. Maria's brother Robert died, perhaps from disease. The wagon train could not afford to wait while the Goulsons dug a grave in the iron-hard ground. If the Goulsons wanted to keep up with the rest of the company, they would have to leave their son. They laid Robert's body on a rock shelf and vowed to come back later to bury him.

ARRIVAL IN FORBESTOWN

Five months and four days after departing Missouri the Goulsons landed at what was known as the old "76" mine in Eureka. From there they went to Chandlerville, but as the year wore on flour and other provisions became so scarce they were compelled to walk out through a murderous winter cold to the larger settlement at Forbestown. They arrived on New Year's Day, 1853, in drifts of snow 20 feet deep.

John Goulson must have had a penchant for new beginnings. When he arrived in Forbestown, he found the settlement was sprouting as fast as a Jimson weed. From its start as a busy trading post with only one hotel on the stage line, it was already evolving into a prospering mining center. The country was rich in gold and quartz deposits and a quartz stamp mill costing over $200,000 was already operating in full swing. By the end of Goulson's first year there, Forbestown had a population of about a thousand people and was second only to Bidwell in size.

Elias Shaw discovered, however, that it was near the end of the peak Gold Rush years in the Mother Lode country. Pea-sized nuggets of the precious metal were no longer just lying in the riverbeds and streams waiting to be picked up. Men had to work much harder—and longer—to make a fortune, and many of them didn't make anything at all. Despite the severe privations the miners endured, the grossly inflated cost of even the bare necessities, and the spontaneous "justice" practiced on the frontier, Elias could see there were plenty of men still pulling wealth out of the ground if they were willing to persevere.

He wasn't afraid of hard work. For the next 14 years Elias applied himself, working the quartz from as far north as La Porte in Plumas County to Forbestown, in what was then Butte County. Elias tried every method of mining gold—placer, hardrock, and hydraulic. He endured days and weeks of back-breaking labor bent over in icy streams, wrenching muscles as he dug deep into the rock. He endured extremes of cold and heat, exhaustion, loneliness, and an endless torment of fleas. At last, his ventures in placer mining were so successful he had enough money to go back to Ohio to buy some fine coach horses, harness, and equipment. He planned to bring them back to California and start a new line of business.

Unfortunately, on the return trip he was robbed. His grandson, John E. Shaw, Jr., tells the story: *"They [Elias and his hired hands] camped in Utah for a few days due to a kick in the stomach by one of his horses. While Elias lay in his tent recuperating from his accident, one of his men was leading the 'Bell Mare' (an older female horse chosen by the other horses as their leader) to water, with the rest of the horses following, when the man was shot through the lower leg by a band of white men dressed as Indians. The Bell Mare (so called by reason of a bell worn around her neck) circled the camp and was leading the horses back to [it] when she was killed by the raiders, stampeding the entire band of horses."* Elias lost everything but the harness and the rest of the trappings he'd purchased. By the time he got back to Forbestown and the Gold Country, he was near broke.

THE GOULSONS LEAVE AND COME BACK AGAIN

Meanwhile, John Goulson had set up a smithy next to a clear-running stream and did brisk business shoeing horses, repairing mining tools, wagons, and wagon wheels. He made more money and in less time at his trade than he would have done by mining. Four years passed and the population of Forbestown grew to about 3,000, including Americans, many foreigners, Mexicans, and a handful of Natives. The town had as many as five hotels and was a vital center that supplied goods and services to several surrounding smaller settlements and over 200 gold digs.

In spite of his success in Forbestown, the 42-year-old Goulson might have begun to feel crowded. Or that the tumultuous, often violent life in the Gold Rush Country threatened his family's future. Whatever the reason, he decided to go back to Wisconsin in 1857. He dreaded retracing the long overland route they had taken to California. Though more expensive, the sea route was reputed to be faster and he could afford it. The Goulsons booked passage on a ship out of San Francisco bound for Panama City, crossed the 50-mile isthmus to Chagres on the Caribbean side, and picked up another ship destined for New York.

Back in Wisconsin, daily life was more civilized and the community more English than it was in Forbestown. Wheat and lumber still dominated the growing state's economy. Augmented by the rapidly emerging dairy industry, and a well-developed rail system that connected passengers and produce to the markets in the East, purses grew fat. All of this made for a dream come true for a skilled blacksmith and John Goulson prospered.

Nine years or so of freezing Midwestern winters passed. Maria's mother, Sarah Haynes Goulson, died [exact date is not known] and John Goulson married another English woman 14 years

Left: *John Goulson and his family, with daughters Maria and Elizabeth standing in back, son Alfred and second wife Annie Wakefield Goulson seated, in Avon, Wisconsin, 1862.*
Above: *The Goulson blacksmith shop in Pescadero. Alfred started working in his father's business in 1881.*

The Shaw Family

his junior named Annie Wakefield. Two more children were born, Maria's half-sister, Elizabeth, and her half-brother Alfred, born on May 6, 1860. Maria grew up and was a teacher in one of the established local public schools for several years.

Events were building in the nation, however, that would again redirect the Goulson family's fate. The Civil War broke out in 1861, a conflict so deep and decisive it divided family members and the minds and hearts of all American citizens for generations to come. Among the many issues that led to the outbreak of war, none was as divisive as slavery. As early as 1854 Wisconsin had demonstrated its alignment with the Union when abolitionists defied the Fugitive Slavery Act. From the initial call for volunteers in 1861 to the war's end in 1865, 96,000 came from Wisconsin to serve, many of them teenagers. The carnage that ensued destroyed families, fortunes and whole cities.

John Goulson had had enough by 1864. Nearly 50 years old, he was weary of the war and the harsh Wisconsin winters. Heartened by the improvements to the trails leading West since he first traveled them, he overcame his reluctance to cross the Plains again. The Goulsons were going back to California.

In the spring the family packed up a wagon, harnessed a mule team, and set out with a company guided by Captain Brooks. Along the way the family revisited the site where they had left the body of John's first son, Robert, but could not find his bones. To the end of her life, Maria remembered her brother with sadness. About four months later—a whole month shorter than their first trip—they reached Virginia City where they stopped to rest before finally going on to resettle at Forbestown.

Reunion in Forbestown

The Goulsons found the town had changed and so had the general character of mining. The glory days of panning and sluicing alluvial gold were coming to an end. The South Feather Water Company that headquartered in Forbestown supplied water to the miners for their placer diggings. Deep quartz mining would eventually take over completely in the coming decades.

Time and fate had brought Elias Shaw and Maria Goulson together again. She was no longer the blacksmith's young daughter he had first become acquainted with crossing the Plains so many years ago. Nor was she the girl he must have glimpsed when the young miner dropped in at her father's shop on supplies-and-repairs runs into Forbestown. Now Maria was a bright, comely woman of 26. Although nearly penniless, Elias was a hard-working man who'd been greatly tempered by experience. John Goulson could recognize integrity when he saw it and was more than happy to renew his friendship with the younger man. He even went so far as to deepen the bond by accepting Elias into the family as Maria's husband.

All of them were ready to move on to a place where life could be sustained more hospitably. John Goulson, his family, and Elias Shaw quit the gold fields forever and went to San Francisco where Elias and Maria were married on October 10, 1866. There they heard of a small town called Pescadero about 50 miles south of the City.

Located in an area rich in timber, farming, and grazing lands, Pescadero had already captured the attention of such San Francisco entrepreneurs as Loren Coburn, who owned a booming livery stable and drayage business in the City. It's very likely that Goulson made Coburn's acquaintance through the mutual interests of their occupations. Coburn was a frankly ambitious capitalist who was busy expanding his personal empire and prospering from the vast tracts of land he was in the process of acquiring down the Coast. Land might still be available and the opportunities for Elias to rebuild his own fortune seemed promising. For Goulson, the advantages were obvious. They moved immediately.

Pescadero — 1866 to 1900s

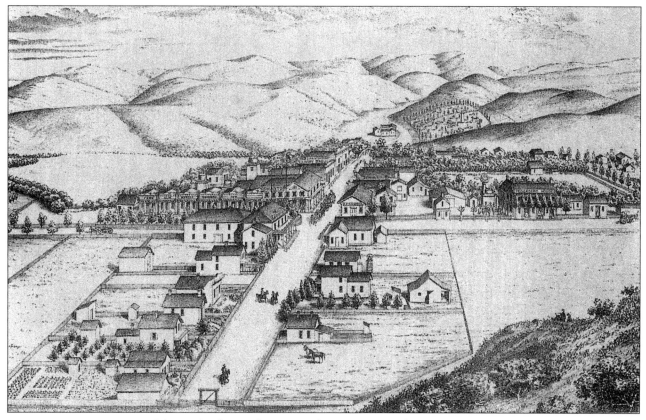

A lithograph of Pescadero, 1878; from A History of San Mateo County.

Pescadero was still an isolated frontier outpost in the northernmost part of Santa Cruz County. Situated over 40 miles away from the county seat, it could only be reached over difficult mountainous terrain on precarious trails in some places no wider than a cow. An annexation movement rumbled as early as 1861 petitioning San Mateo County for inclusion, but the town wouldn't become part of San Mateo County for another two years after the Goulsons and Shaws arrived.

In spite of its remoteness, Pescadero was a newly blossoming township. In the 13 years since Alex Moore started building the first frame house, it had grown in size from an adobe dwelling attended by a few outlying buildings into a small village of New England-style frame houses. Bristling with energy, Pescadero was the hub of even tinier communities—mostly scattered rural households and mill operations—in an area roughly defined by Punta del Año Nuevo to the south; Tunitas to the north; La Honda, several miles back in the eastern hills; and the Pacific Ocean.

According to the 1860 Santa Cruz County census there were 428 "free" inhabitants in the district, not counting an abundance of grizzly bears. The majority of men worked as farmers and farm laborers, woodsmen, and seamen. And in town there were businesses: four blacksmiths; four butchers; five carpenters; a couple of bricklayers; one doctor; and a saloonkeeper. A stage service started up between Pescadero and Half Moon Bay the year the Goulsons and Shaws arrived and by

Edward Washburn Weeks Collection.

the next year a second was running daily that connected with San Mateo through La Honda.

The Swanton House offered fine hotel accommodations, and had already set a standard of country elegance for locals and guests who came to Pescadero to hunt, fish, and relax that would last over the next six decades. Fraternal orders and churches were firmly rooted, too. The Independent Order of Good Templars had organized the year before the Goulsons and Shaws arrived and the Methodist Episcopal Church fellowship, which was the first to hold services in town, was followed soon after by the Congregational Church and St. Anthony's Catholic Church. Pescadero had even established a library from contributions made by its citizens.

In the years after the Civil War ended, the country went into a period of turmoil and eventual collapse that culminated in the nationwide financial panic of 1872. A long depression followed, but Pescadero folks managed to hold on in spite of it. During the '70s and '80s the growth of the town paralleled that of the dairy business on the Coast. Besides the

82   Portraits of Pescadero

dairies operating in the hills and flats around Pescadero, the Steele family established themselves, first renting much of Loren Coburn's Año Nuevo land, and then buying it. Agriculture and milling were also thriving. If you lived on a farm or worked timber in the forest, you would always eat.

Petroleum was gradually replacing fuel oil previously gotten by whaling. The whaling industry's gradual decline impacted Pescadero's Portuguese community in particular, even though heavy immigration from the Azores continued to bring more and more Portuguese to the Coast. These resourceful people turned to dairy farming and soon excelled at it. By the end of the 1870s the Portuguese community in Half Moon Bay [Spanishtown] was big enough to start the Chamarita Festival (Feast of the Holy Ghost). Pescadero's Portuguese went to Half Moon Bay until 1900 when they brought the celebration home to their own chapel. From then on, when Chamarita time came, the town's brass band would crank up, mothers pinned flowers to their hats, and children struggled not to squirm in their best clothes as the whole town turned out for the parade through town and the feast that took place afterwards.

By 1878 Pescadero had developed from a village into a small but full-fledged township, boasting a miller, a blacksmith, livery stables, shoemakers, a meat market, two doctors, two hotels and four mercantile stores. Social life centered on the school, the churches, and a number of the town's more recently established fraternal organizations such as the International Order of Oddfellows and the Independent Order of Good Templars. The library was still going strong and considered to be one of the best in San Mateo County.

Construction was booming, both in town and in the surrounding district. St. Anthony's was the town's second church to be built, serving community members of the Catholic faith. It was finished in 1870 and embellished by a beautiful bell tower in the late '80s. The first public schoolhouse—a beautifully designed two-story building—rose up proudly in the lot next door to St. Anthony's. Not to be outdone, the Methodist Episcopalians at last were able to build a church of their own in 1889, raising the number of Protestant denominations in town to two. For a population of 200 to 300 town residents, this was pretty good. The Methodist Episcopalians couldn't hold on longer than 15 years, however. When they ran out of money and preachers they abandoned their building to community use. Down at Pigeon Point, the lighthouse dedicated in 1872 made it safer for both passenger and cargo ships

Opposite page:
Above: *An 1890s' scene of the crossroads at Pescadero. The Swanton House is on the right; across the street from it is the Levy Brothers store.*
Below: *One of the original stagecoaches that ran the route to Pescadero, currently housed at the historical museum in Santa Ynez (Solvang), California.*

Patricia McCormick Dougherty Collection.

This page, above:
The Congregational Church was built in 1867. Interestingly, the Articles of Faith were written by seven people of wide religious persuasion—two Baptists, one Moravian, a Dutch Reformist; and Mr. and Mrs. Samuel Besse were Methodists. The only one of them who was actually a Congregationalist was Mrs. J.C. Badger, Barzillai Hayward's widowed sister. She later married Mr. M.R. Ellis, one of the ministers of the Church.

This is the back of present-day North Street ("Irish Row"). In the center of the picture is St. Anthony's Church and to its left, the original grammar school designed by John McKay.

to ply the treacherous seas between Monterey to San Francisco without wrecking, but the hope of a safe shipping port located close to town died when Gordon's Chute at Tunitas was destroyed by fire in 1885 and never rebuilt.

In the '80s the Southern Pacific Railroad carried passengers and goods from San Francisco to San Mateo and Redwood City and from these points stagecoaches ran 30 miles over the hills to Pescadero. The Simon Knight stage line serviced town twice daily, one coach connecting from Searsville to San Gregorio through La Honda, and the other through Half Moon Bay. Townspeople were also in touch with the world by telegraph and mail was delivered to their own post office. Pescadero folks really knew they were on the map when the Swanton House had become so famous it was listed as a "California Resort" in an 1884 edition of *Appleton's General Guide to United States and Canada*!

It wasn't until the 1890s that Pescadero felt the bite of hunger that the rest of the nation had experienced in the '70s. The decade started off in January 1890 with a "very big flood" in Pescadero. The townspeople shook it off, because floods were normal occurrences, but some people reflecting upon it later might have seen it as an omen of the darker times ahead. In 1894 Democrat Grover Cleveland was elected president of the United States and, according to the Shaws' hired hand, Frank George, the next four years of his term marked the "worst Depression of all times."

In Pescadero, people who didn't live directly off their own land were especially hard up. The town relied on the sound character of its citizens to get by. Frank George recalled that J.C. Williamson and the Levy Brothers stores "fed a multitude of people during the depression of 1894 to 1898. And Mr. Williamson was making such a go of the store because he had all the cash customers while Levy's had all credit customers." Williamson's generosity helped to support people's livelihoods and in some cases their fortunes. Looking back at this time, Louise Williamson later remarked that "...when he died, some of the Portuguese people came to see him and one man said, 'This is the godfather to the poor.' He helped people with their reading, writing, and banking without taking any money—they used to have to go to Redwood City for their banking. Everyone had great confidence in him."

84 Portraits of Pescadero

Chamarita in Pescadero

In the top picture, the Festival of the Holy Ghost parade with its queens and attendants halts in front of St. Anthony's Catholic Church on North Street. They will be starting back to the bridge, hanging a left, and marching back to the I.D.E.S. hall where the feast is waiting for them. Ca. early 1900s.

Behind the procession, the town band waits in front of St. Anthony's church. The town's first grammar schoolhouse can be seen in the background.

In the photograph at the bottom, the famous Pescadero brass brand is getting ready to march and play. The man with the "X" over his head is Frank George; he played horn.

Williamson's store was a town institution. The Native Sons of the Golden West met in the hall upstairs; the stage stopped regularly here, as did the mail, and the Fireman's Fund was next door.

In Frank George's opinion, things started to look up again in 1898 when Republican William McKinley was elected to the country's highest executive office.

Pescadero's reputation as a resort continued to grow. The fishing was fine; nearby Pebble Beach was an ideal place to picnic and hunt for semi-precious stones; the Coastal weather was cool when the inland was hot. Although Pescadero's first automobile would not appear until 1924, people who lived in the cities were buying them as fast as they could afford them and spent their holidays motoring down the road in search of quieter places.

Local dreamers were investing in The Ocean Shore Railway Company, incorporated in 1905, with plans to capitalize on the greater flow of tourists and goods that would come through Pescadero by the trainload. Building began at both ends of the proposed line simultaneously—San Francisco and Santa Cruz—and significant work laying rail had begun when the 1906 earthquake struck. The quake obliterated much of the grade dug at Pedro Point and Devil's Slide, dumping heavy equipment into the ocean. Although grading was resumed the following year, the trains eventually never ran farther than Tunitas to the north of Pescadero, or Davenport to the south, leaving the town stranded in the middle of a 26-mile gap.

The April 18 earthquake that took San Francisco down also affected Pescadero. In her notes, Grace Shaw remembered the quake was "so strong it knocked down all the chimneys in town." Then, just as townspeople were sufficiently recovered from the shock to put their homes back together again, there was another big flood in Pescadero on May 6. The hardy Pescaderans took adversity in stride and their independent way of life went on, much as it had before.

ELIAS SHAW FAMILY — 1866

When Elias and Maria Shaw arrived in Pescadero they set up their first household at what was known as Shaw's Camp in the forested hills of the Little Bútano, part of a former Mexican land grant that Loren Coburn now owned. John Goulson built his own blacksmith shop in Pescadero town and plied his trade until he retired a couple of decades later. At Shaw Camp, Elias felled redwood trees and cut them down into bolts that he then sold to a local shingle mill. After a couple of years he was ready to get out of the lumbering business and take up the occupation he'd grown up with. He returned to farming.

The Shaws—Elias, Maria, and their first-born child, Annie—left Bútano Canyon in 1868 to rent and operate various farms in the Pescadero area over the next 13 years. Four more children were born during this time: Edgar in 1869, and Bertha, born August 13, 1872, both in Pescadero; Grace, in 1875, at Pomponio; and John Elias Shaw, October 5, 1877, in town.

In 1874 Elias Shaw purchased a 300-acre farm from Aaron Honsinger, an Ohio man who'd arrived in Pescadero the same year as the Shaws, but Elias rented the land out to other people until 1881 when the family moved there to live. Their ranch lay about a mile northeast of town amid farmlands owned by Honsinger, B.V. Weeks, Thomas and Alex Moore, and Lafe Chandler; one of the nearby properties was rented by the Adair family and later, the Mattei family became neighbors, too. Elias and Maria's last two children, twins Charles Evans and James Goulson Shaw, were born at home in late July 1882. After Elias Shaw's death in 1894, Edgar and John Shaw, Sr. ran the ranch under the name of Shaw Bros. In 1908 they bought more of the adjoining land, bringing their total holdings to more than 500 acres.

Maria's younger half-brother Alfred Goulson went to work as an apprentice in his father's blacksmith shop when he was 21, the same year the Shaws moved to their ranch. He married a girl he'd grown up with in Pescadero, Aaron Honsinger's daughter Jessie, on October 1, 1887 and carried on his father's trade well into the late 1920s. Maria's half-sister, Elizabeth, married Ben Pinkham, a native of Maine, and lived in town.

John Goulson nearly lived to see his 80th birthday, passing on just a few days short of it on April 7, 1895. His wife, Annie, survived him for another 19 years. Both now lie in the Mount Hope cemetery in Pescadero.

JOHN SHAW AND RUTH BALDWIN – 1911

Sometime during 1908 a young lady named Ruth Baldwin would come down from San Francisco with her sisters, Jean and Gertrude, to visit with their friend Margaret Chandler (Lafe Chandler's second wife) in Pescadero. On one of these occasions she made the acquaintance of Elias and Maria Shaw's son, John Elias Shaw. John was taken with this magnetically charming woman. Portraits taken of her from the period show an honest face with a broad forehead, eyes that looked out at the world with interest, and a rounded chin set on a firm jaw that hinted at a determined spirit. At 33, John was a good prospect, too. Handsome and hard-working, he came from a good family and lived on his own land. He could tell a good story and was not above barbing one or two with an earthy sense of humor. Ruth fell for him. They went off to San Francisco and got married in January of 1911, then honeymooned at Mt. Tamalpais. The honeymoon probably didn't last too long because as it was the heavy milking season John was anxious to get back to his dairy at Shaw Ranch.

For Ruth, life on a dairy ranch must have been very different from life in the city. Self-reliance was the rule. Daily activities were governed by the demands of work and the weather. The well-being of the family depended upon the well-being of their crops and milk cows. And even though there were occa- *(Continued on page 90)*

Excerpts from

The Diary of Bertha Shaw, 1883-1884
San Mateo Historical Museum Archives, Manuscript 66-127

It's hard to read Bertha's handwriting on some of the diary's pages where erasures or smudges blur the pencil marks. But the 10-year-old's observations are lively and clear. In the excerpts that follow, she gives us an insight into what daily life was like a year or so after the family moved onto their own land at Shaw Ranch.

January 1, 1883. It snows a little. For Christmas, Bertha receives a hat; two books, one called *Alladin* and the other, *Chatterbox*; a pair of stockings; a basket of flowers; a handkerchief; and lots of candy and nuts. A few days later she gets a pair of gloves and a metal pencil.

There are nine in the family: Mama [43], Papa [55], and seven children, two of whom are twins Charlie and Jim, born July 28, 1882. Every month Bertha records how old they are. She and her younger sister Grace tend the babies when Mama needs to rest.

Bertha's older sister Annie [16] and brother Edgar [14] regularly do the wash about once a week. This chore usually takes half a day. Annie does the ironing the day after. Bertha is making a patchwork.

Weather is an important subject. If it is bad, it's "disagreeable;" if it is good, it's "pleasant." She observes the wind closely—how strong it is, which direction it blows. On **January 10** she says they see a comet every night when they go to bed. During the winter months there are many days of frost, cold, rain, and wind, with occasional fine days when it is warm and clear. As the year progresses and typical Coastal weather patterns set in, more and more days are "foggie."

Bertha Shaw, as a young woman.

One day she and the others dress up in ferns, leaves and little berries. After a frost, the kids go back to school and the cow calves.

John Beeding has a fishpond that is "…awful deep. …They say Mr. Beeding caught his death of cold making it and he hung his self." A few weeks later Bertha reports that Mr. Beeding is doing poorly, so it seems he didn't actually die by hanging. [*Franklin* Beeding died June 6, 1883.]

When the "menfolks" go hunting, their luck is often astonishing: Edgar catches 11 quail in one day, and 29 the next; later in the year, her father bags a large number of rabbits. Bertha is disgusted. She doesn't like cleaning the animals they bring home.

Farm work is divided up. "Papa serving barley all day; James and Sam harrowing. Ben is making gates." When the season is right, the kids pick berries and go fishing. Bertha catches "8 beauties" one time. Later in May, when lots of little fish are in the creek, the girls go wading; their chaperone, Miss Thompson, sits in the grove.

Jan. 21, 1883: George Adair and Nettie come up to visit. Today is [cannot read] Adair's birthday. Bertha spends the night at Lizzie Chrisman's. [Since people lived far apart, they usually made the most of their time together by extending their visits to one- or two-night stays. The girls—especially Annie, who is older—do this whenever they can.]

Jan. 28, 1883: "Those people down to New Year's Island have a little boy." [She records several births, illnesses, and deaths.]

At school, girls play jump rope; boys have great fun playing ball and football [soccer].

Feb. 6, 1883: Chinese New Year. Bertha stays home from school, sick. Their neighbor's new baby is so sick it is expected to die. The baby does die in a few days.

Feb. 14, 1883: Valentines are exchanged and Bertha is pleased to get at least one.

Washington's Birthday is a big holiday. Everybody in town goes to the beach and has such a good time they call off school for the next day, too.

Mar. 8, 1883: Bertha complains: "Exams [at school] today very hard."

St. Patrick's Day is celebrated; on **Apr. 1, 1883**, Bertha gets fooled.

Apr. 10, 1883: Bertha goes to town with Annie and Edgar where they hear of four men who drowned Sunday (it had been raining heavily for some time). "It was Frank Pratt, Clayton Pratt, Mr. Ashley and Mr. Collren [lighthouse keepers]....They had wives and children." None of the bodies are found until nearly a month later. "It was Frank Pratt. He was found up by Pigen [sic] Point. They could not tell who he was only by the boot he had on. One of his legs and head was gone."

Apr. 12, 1883: Grace and Bertha go up to Wurr Mill with Tilda. "It is 22 miles there and back. Grandma and Grandpa [Goulson] came home with us."

Apr. 16, 1883: Jim and Edgar are making a garden; birds are nesting.

May 20, 1883: Bee swarms. (Also the next day.) George Adair, wife and baby visit.

May 23, 1883: "It is the hottest day we have yet this year. Mr. Hughs gave me one of those Japinis perisols [sic]."

Feb. 24, 1884: David Moore and Mary Hayward get married.

First published in 1878, Chatterbox *was a popular children's magazine containing a wide range of stories, history and geography lessons, practical science experiments, and pictures.*

(Continued from page 87) sional social events and friends in town, Ruth's new life in the country meant that relationships outside of the immediate family circle were precious. Neighbors did not live next door—they lived on the next ranch, which was sometimes many miles away. Companionship came while sharing chores that needed to be done and facing crises together when something went wrong.

At the time Ruth and John married, the warm center of the mostly masculine Shaw household was Maria Shaw, then a 70-year-old widow. Maria must have helped to smooth out the rough edges

Ruth Baldwin. Ca. 1900.

Newlyweds Ruth and John Shaw on Shaw Ranch. 1911.

Maria Goulson Shaw in 1911. She is 71 years old.

for her new daughter-in-law, helping her adjust to washing clothes by hand and making bread from scratch. Her kindness and strength were legend in Pescadero. People loved to hear of Maria's girlhood adventures crossing oceans and continents, her stories of Vigilante Days and the gold mining camps, and her recollections of the great Civil War. Ruth must have taken great comfort from the older woman's knowledge and enduringness.

Of Maria's seven children, only three still lived and worked on the ranch: John; his older brother Edgar, a bachelor; and their unmarried sister, Grace Shaw, whose health was not strong. Frank George, their hired man, worked side by side with the brothers every day and had been with them so long he was practically part of the family.

The rest were gone. Annie Shaw had been married to Daniel Adair for over 15 years and lived with him and their three children in Pescadero town. Bertha Shaw had moved even farther away to

Santa Cruz with her husband, Ben Blaisdell. The twins, Charlie and Jim, had both married and were raising their families in San Francisco.

Ruth rolled up her sleeves. She learned how to manage meals and hygiene without the benefit of city amenities. And before long, she began raising children, for just about the time Ruth was getting the hang of country living, the Shaws' first son, John Elias Shaw, Jr., was born on December 21, 1911. Carol Gertrude Shaw followed in less than a year, the day after Thanksgiving, 1912. With two young babies in hand, Ruth and John gave themselves a short break and

Top: *Bertha and Edgar Shaw show off the results of a deer-hunting expedition. 1917.*

Bottom: *On the left, Ruth and Burns the dog with the Shaws' first baby, John Elias Shaw Jr. It is a winter day in late December 1911. On the right, Edgar, John Sr. (holding John Jr.), and neighbor Kelly Mattei. 1911-12.*

Timeline 1880 – 1900
Highlighted parallel events in San Francisco Bay Area, California, and the Nation

1880 As the proportion of Chinese migrant laborers in California grows, wages are driven down and Americans resent them more and more.

The San Mateo County census records 238 people in Pescadero; 26 in San Gregorio.

1881 James A. Garfield, Republican, is inaugurated as President but serves only six months before he is assassinated on September 17, 1881. Chester A. Arthur replaces him and serves out the rest of the term.

1882 The Chinese Exclusion Act is passed. Japanese immigration begins.

1885 After centuries of isolation, the Japanese government allows male workers to emigrate to Hawai'i and the Coast as field workers. In the next 40 years about 380,000 Japanese people immigrate.

Grover Cleveland, Democrat, is sworn in on March 4, 1885 to serve one term as President.

1887 The General Allotment Act eliminates collective tribal land ownership by Native peoples in America.

In California the Wright Act permits regions to form and bond irrigation districts, the single most important contribution to the growth of state agriculture.

1889 Republican Benjamin Harrison becomes President and serves one term.

AN ADVERTISEMENT FOR THE MIDWINTER EXPOSITION IN SAN FRANCISCO, 1894, FROM GRACE SHAW'S MEMORY ALBUM.

1890s California bcomes the nation's window on the Pacific. At the beginning of the decade there are 107,000 Chinese and 2,039 Japanese in the state.

1890 Yosemite National Park Bill is pushed through Congress.

The San Mateo County census records 221 people in Pescadero.

1892 The Sierra Club is incorporated in San Francisco on June 4, co-founded by John Muir.

Democrat Grover Cleveland is elected president and serves for one term.

1897 Republican William McKinley takes office as President. He is re-elected in 1900 but serves only five months before he is assassinated on September 14, 1901. The Vice President and Assistant Secretary of the Navy, Theodore Roosevelt, takes charge.

1898 The United States takes possession of Puerto Rico and the Philippine Islands; it also annexes the Hawaiian Islands.

The first automobile in the state is owned by W.L. Elliott in Oakland.

waited until March 10, 1914 to have Ruth Mary Shaw. A fourth child, Elaine Baldwin Shaw, arrived on October 10, 1916. Life at the Shaw Ranch was grand.

Then the Shaws' happy marriage was cut tragically short. After only eight years together with John, Ruth died unexpectedly on April 12, 1919, six months before she turned 37, while giving birth to their fifth child at Mills Hospital. The infant boy died with her. The shock of this loss was so great it may have precipitated Maria Shaw's death. A month later, she was gone too.

ELAINE BALDWIN SHAW

Elaine was two-and-a-half years old when her mother and grandmother died. Her brother and sisters were very young, too: John, the oldest, was 7-1/2; Carol, 6-1/2; and Ruth, 5. It was too much for their Aunt Grace to deal with, being the only woman left at home and often feeling poorly. Their grieving father hired housekeepers to take care of the kids and help run the household while he and Edgar managed the work on the ranch. Elaine recalls:

"*My father hired housekeepers from San Francisco. He'd look in the San Francisco Examiner and call them up; he went up and got them in the horse and buggy.*

"*We had a terrific turn-over. Then we finally got this old German lady. Mrs. Hauck, her name was. We called her 'Haucky.' She was very strict, but she taught us. She used to say, 'I'll knock your g-d head off!' and my father would get mad at her. Once she gave me such a licking, he fired her right then, but I guess he forgave her.*

"*We all had chores to do. There was lots of work: She had to make bread; she had to wash by hand; cook on a wood stove. She was a wonderful cook. She stayed seven years with us. Then Mrs. Hauck got high blood pressure or something and she had to go back to San Francisco to live with her son and daughter-in-law.*"

After Mrs. Hauck's departure, Elaine's older sister Carol, only 13 or 14, took over the primary household responsibilities.

"*Of course Mrs. Hauck had taught Carol how to cook, but poor Carol. I can remember her telling me in later years how she'd sit in the last period in high school—English class—wondering, 'What am I going to cook for dinner?' Carol was good cooking on the wood stove, and washing by hand—but not making bread, because we could buy bread in Pescadero then.*"

Everyone pitched in. By the time John turned 12 he was getting up early every morning to help milk the cows. Elaine remembers that Ruth was in charge of the bedroom; Elaine liked being out-

"*We had a good, a happy life. We were all very close. My father always said, 'If one did something, the other never told.' We were very close, my brother, my sisters and I. We never told on one another. We all took the blame, I guess.*"

Elaine, Carol, John, and Ruth at a Pebble Beach picnic. July 4, 1919.

The Shaw Family 93

side, so she picked apples and vegetables, brought in wood and made sure the wood box was filled.

"We had to help one another. One of my horrible chores [laughs]… Carol, my sister, she was very exacting; everything had to be just right. She was four years older; I was about 9. My sister Ruth—the middle girl—on Saturday, she had to change the beds and sweep. We had board floors—we didn't have linoleum or anything, it was pine floor—she'd sweep and mop the floors. Carol did all the dishes that we didn't do during the week. You know, the mush—the cereal dishes—would stick and they'd go under the sink until Saturday. She didn't have Chore Boys, or SOS or anything, and she'd scrub those. I had to wipe dishes. Then she'd put the washing on, in the big boiler on the wood stove, and get the heat going, especially for the white clothes. Then you'd have to carry them out to the porch and put them in the stationary tubs. She washed all the white clothes and the colored clothes but she saved all my Dad's and my brother's overalls for me. I got all those horrible things. The water was half cold. Then you had to have room to hang them out.

"Carol had to get lunch, you know, a big lunch; she always baked beans on Saturday. We had beans a lot.

Above: Back row, standing: John Sr. and wife Ruth; Charlie Shaw; Ben Blaisdell; Annie Shaw Adair; Jim Shaw; Dan Adair. Front, seated: Nellie Shaw (Charlie's wife); Bertha Shaw Blaisdell; Minnie Shaw (Jim's wife).
Below, left: Ben Blaisdell with Bertha and Miriam Adair.
Below, right: At a beach picnic, Grace Shaw on the left with Bertha and Miriam Adair; Ben Blaisdell is standing in back, at left; Annie and Dan Adair (in captain's hat) seated on right.

94 *Portraits of Pescadero*

And of course we had cheese and butter and milk from the farm, because we had a little cheese factory. They made their own California cheddar, a yellow cheese. It was delicious.

"After lunch we had to scrub the dining room and the kitchen floors because they'd be greasy and dirty and muddy. Carol melted the crystal light bar soap on the stove some way. You shaved a little bit to make liquid soap that you threw around so you could scrub. Then you had to rinse that all off.

"Sometimes Carol and Ruth'd get into it. You know, they were both just so tired. And she'd say, 'Ruth! Get the hell out!' [chuckles] And of course Elaine had to take over and help her finish. Usually when she and Ruth got along all right—which they did most of the time—it was always my job [to rinse off] the old porch. Then we'd air out the house and it'd be clean as a whistle for the weekend and the week.

"…There was wood to get in, kindling to chop. Because my brother worked with the men, I had to carry the wood in to this big wood box, chop kindling. Chopped my fingers once in a while. We had chickens; we had to hunt the eggs and feed the chickens…

"My father had a garden. He always raised a lot of onions and I used to help him do that. Some of the time they raised green peas; we'd have to pick peas, which was hard work.

"I remember my sister Ruth and I, when we were older, in high school, I guess—it was after my father was gone and my uncle and my brother were running the ranch—they had us picking peas. I remember I had an ulcerated tooth and I felt so sick, picking these peas. I think they paid us a dollar a sack to pick. It was like a grain sack. When they shipped them to market they got 50 cents a sack. [laughs] I don't think we got paid very much. That's just the way the times were."

Ben Blaisdell and his wife, Bertha, had no children of their own, but both delighted in the offspring of their brothers and sisters. In many family pictures Ben is seen having fun with the kids at the ranch. Above, Ben, Carol and John Shaw Jr. pose with a fine catch of fish. Below, Ben gives nieces a "pony" ride. Dan Adair pulls a daughter on the sled while Annie and an unidentified lady look on.

MEMORIES OF FATHER / BROTHER JOHN

"I was a tomboy and I loved to be outside. I loved my father, as we all did, and he taught me to ride. He always saddled the horse [for me], but one day he said, 'I'm going to show you one last time. I'm not going to always be here for you. You have to learn how do it yourself.' In the summer the men would be out binding grain, cutting hay and things like that, and when it came 3 or 3:30, it was up to Elaine to get the cows in. We had about 60 head of dairy cattle, and they pastured in daytime up on several acres in back of us. It wasn't hard, because I rode the horse and they wanted to come home and be milked. That was fun. I loved doing that.

"My brother got up early at 4 o'clock in the morning, to get the cows and milk them. In June, soon as school got out for the summer, we girls would get up about 5 and walk down into (Continued on page 99)

Excerpted from Oral Histories of : Walter H. Moore; Louise Moore Williamson; and

Frank George

San Mateo Historical Museum Archives, Transcript 78-218
taken by Pat Bouris and Elsie Gorski for Spanishtown Historical Society, 11/13/1973

Frank George's father emigrated from the Azores when he was about 23 years old. Just before moving to Pescadero in 1877, he married an Azorean woman, Mary Jesus Freitas, up at Alameda.

"Father became a citizen as soon as he was eligible. He felt there was no place like America. He was a mariner and sailed all over the world, I guess. In those days, the young men had to serve in the military [in Portugal] but many would skip out before the time came to serve. My dad did that but later when he returned to the [Azores] islands to visit his folks, the authorities nabbed him and put him in jail. A few days later, the captain noticed a man missing and when it was discovered it was my father, the captain took an American flag, went up to the authorities, put the flag on my dad and said, 'This is my man and I am taking him with me.' Which he did and that's how my father got back."

Frank George Sr. worked at a whaling station and then at Gazos Mills for the McKinley Brothers, where young Frank was born on July 4, 1884. "The sawmill was so far up, they brought the lumber down in trolleys. I [young Frank] quit after the mule sit-down. Henry Dearborn who owned Dearborn Park was a foreman of the McKinley Brothers at that time. [I worked for Charles McKinley, President William McKinley's brother.] The women folks were working in the woods a long way from there. My mother and Mrs. Dearborn had cabins close together and once Mrs. Dearborn's chimney caught fire which was two days before I was born. They got a ladder and Mrs. Dearborn got on the roof while my mother packed the water and together they put out the fire. Mrs. Dearborn was with my mother when I was born and my mother was with her when one of her sons was born."

Frank says that his father always voted Republican. "From 1894 to 1898 was the worst depression of all time. I've been through several but that was the worst. Grover Cleveland was president and the Democrats in power those four years didn't believe in tariffs, but in free trade. Our markets were closed—but those that were open were flooded with foreign goods. You could buy the best woolen suits for $12 but no one had that kind of money to pay for it. Also, one could buy the best cow in the country but no money to pay for it. Dairymen had hundreds of calves and couldn't sell them even though they were offered for 25 cents. So they were fed to the pigs. Everything had stopped. In 1898 William McKinley [a Republican] was elected and even before taking office, things picked up. Wheels started turning, factories opened up and foreign goods were kept out and then we had prosperity. It was said that the Republican Party would always give us prosperity."

Frank went to Pescadero Elementary School as far as the seventh grade; in 1898, his father died when Frank was only 11 or 12 years old. His mother was left with six children and no

The men get up hay on the Shaw Ranch. Ben Blaisdell and Frank George, in a white shirt, are atop the hay pile. Charlie and Jim Shaw are raking in front of the Petaluma baling machine. 1908.

income. As there were "too many mouths to feed" Frank helped out. He lived at home in town and went to work for the Shaw brothers up at their dairy ranch. It was the beginning of a long relationship.

House in Pescadero: *"My home was one of the first built in Pescadero. It's 105 years old [built in 1868]. Mrs. Louise Williamson's grandfather's sister married a man named John Besse and they bought the ranch right next to Alexander Moore. He built my home for his father and mother."*

Fun: *"We used to have a Fourth of July picnic. The biggest one we had was in 1906, right after the earthquake. Mrs. Williamson's father was a great promoter; he got busy and said that we would have a great celebration, and so he got contributions from all over the county. The day of the picnic there were firemen here and a parade that went clear around the block. The town was full of people."*

Church and the Pescadero Cemetery: Frank went to St. Anthony's Catholic Church. He was baptized in 1884 with four of his father's friends to witness. They were sailors, like his father. There was a bell on a platform outside the church that the priest struck on special occasions.

"Babies generally cry and raise thunder when being baptized, but I laughed when they did that." John Bennet, one of his father's friends, saw him laughing and went outside to ring the bell. When the priest asked Bennet why, he said, *"I want everyone to know we are baptizing a mariner's son this day."*

Frank George worked at the Shaw Ranch for 27 years and knew the family as well as he knew his own. Nearly a lifetime went by, however, before he married Grace Shaw. By 1936—the middle of the Depression—John Elias Shaw Sr., Edgar, James, Annie, and her husband Daniel Adair had all died. Charlie lived in San Francisco, John Jr. down the Coast, and Bertha and her husband Ben Blaisdell in Santa Cruz. Carol, Ruth, and Elaine were all married and gone, too. Then Frank lost his mother in 1939. Although Stanley Steele worked at the Shaw Ranch by then, he lived with his family down at Año Nuevo. Grace—still a maiden lady—was practically alone on the ranch except for Frank. It seemed only right that they honor their long friendship by marrying.

Grace Shaw died in 1956; Frank, in 1974. Close companions still, they lie next to each other at Mt. Hope Cemetery in Pescadero.

To feed their dairy cows, the Shaws—like everyone else in the Pescadero community—shared labor and machinery to get the job done in a narrow time frame. Above, the men on the Shaw Ranch are baling hay using the Moore threshing machine. At the left, Frank George and John Shaw Sr. work together on the Petaluma hay press. 1908.

The next generation worked just as hard, and often with fewer hands. At right, John Jr. runs the grain binder on Shaw Ranch. July 23, 1934.

Left: *John Shaw Jr. with five heifers in the hills above the Shaw Ranch. (Early 1920s)*

Top: *John Shaw Sr. and his brother, Edgar, were good-humored men.*

Above: *Uncle Edgar was a shy man. When he was older, he had a woman friend named Betty Gordon, a nurse who had taken care of him when he was laid up for a long time. When she was 14 Elaine came in the house one day to find Edgar and Betty sitting on the couch, with Edgar's arm around her. Elaine was shocked—at his age! Her uncle's hair was white already! Afterwards Betty came to visit the house periodically, sometimes staying for a week at a time.*

Here's Betty with Elaine, out for a ride on August 14, 1934.

(Continued from page 95) what was called the 'Slough' to pick blackberries. It was about a mile away; most of it was on Mattei's ranch, but we bordered over the fence. We'd take 10-pound water buckets and fill our lard buckets and be back in time to get breakfast. That was a job, but it was fun. We'd eat, we'd fill our tummies before breakfast—we didn't even have breakfast when we left. Then we'd come back and have blackberries and sugar and all this wonderful cream. [chuckles] You'd think we'd been sick of berries, but we weren't. It was so good.

"John had a pet cow named Patty. When they'd go out in the morning to let the cows out, John would hop on her and she'd buck and buck. John was a good rider, he didn't have any surcingle or anything. One time they got Hale—my cousin from San Francisco—on her. My father tapped her on the seat and she started bucking. Hale, of course, went head over heels and landed in a cow flop. It was springtime, and it was kind of juicy. He was a big boy, about 14, but he went home crying to his mother. She was so mad at my father.

"My father loved to play jokes. He got caught up one time [when] we invited Miss Geisendorfer [a teacher at school] up to ride horseback. We had olive trees. You know the olives, you can't pick them and eat them, they're tart…bitter…and that was one of his favorite things. He'd take somebody over to the orchard and hand them an olive. Of course they'd spit and sputter. It was horrible…fresh olives, you know. Well, he gave one to Miss Geisendorfer. She took that olive, spit the pit out, chewed it up and swallowed it and never made a face. Never said a thing. He got quiet. [laughs]"

Elaine started high school not long after the onset of the Great Depression. Because the family farmed their own place, and had always been accustomed to relying on themselves to provide for their needs, perhaps they didn't suffer as much as city folks who

John Elias Shaw Sr. died in 1932, a much-beloved member of the Pescadero community. For many years he served as a trustee for Pescadero's high school. The notice in the school paper, The Carnelian, marked his passing with this verse:

Hound and Horn
Hound and horn are on the hill.
Then all is still.

Over the ridge above the town
A mist comes down: —

A white mist veiling field and sky
To the hunter's eye;

Wind and rain blow thru the grass
Where he should pass;

Softly the evening shadows fall,
And then the call:

"Hound and horn are on the hill."
Then all is still.
— [Edwin Willimen, Principal]

IN MEMORY OF JOHN E. SHAW
1877 – 1932

had no way of raising their own food or country folks who owned no land. Still, cash was hard to come by.

"DITCH DAY" AT PESCADERO HIGH SCHOOL

"It was May 1st and trout season opened. All four of us were in high school—my brother was a senior. He and Earle Williamson and a lot of the boys went up to the Honsinger Ranch because Earle Williamson had a few head of cattle and they had themselves a little rodeo up there. You could look down on them from the Shaw ranch. My father was out checking cows or something and he saw all this activity down there. He almost went down, but he had to get back to do something so he didn't, thank goodness. In the meantime, Elaine and Frances Weeks, a Japanese boy who had a truck—I can't remember how many of us—we went. I just walked out with them. Carol stayed at school and didn't get into it. I was a freshman! Imagine, having that much nerve!

"We went down where there was a pool, like Lake Lucerne, and a little dam. Joe Takata left us off and went up to get the boys. We didn't have any swimming suits but we just left our brassieres and panties on and got in the water. When Joe and the boys came back, here we were—we had to stay in the water! [laughing] We couldn't get out!

"And the worst part was, the 'credibility inspector' from UC came that day to the high school. Harriet [Williamson] and Patty McCormick wanted to go to UC and they cried because they knew the school wouldn't be accredited since half the student body wasn't there. I can't remember how we got home and all.

"Dad had kind of a fiery temper and I didn't know what was going to happen. Carol said, 'You have to tell Dad what you did.' She said, 'I'm not going to tell him. You have to tell him.'

"I used to get up and help my father and my brother feed calves in the morning, so when I went down the next morning to feed the calves, I got up nerve enough and told him that I had ditched school the day before. I think he uttered a couple of cuss words and said, 'If you don't want to go to school,'—they were ripping off the wallpaper and putting in wallboard—'you can stay home and rip off wallpaper.' And that's all he said. I got off lucky. He went to the [school] trustee meeting that night, I guess, and he had heard all about it. I guess John had to confess, too. I got out of that one. Ha! Purely lucky."

Early in 1932 when Elaine was 15, her father died. This sorrow added even greater hardship to the family's daily life. A year and a half later, Elaine graduated in the class of 1933 from Pescadero Union High School. She wanted to continue her education, but as her older sisters were moving away from the family

100 Portraits of Pescadero

home and into their own adult lives, Elaine was faced with the practical necessity of taking on more responsibility at Shaw Ranch by helping her Aunt Grace.

First Car / Electricity [1930s]

"I was taking [Aunt Grace] to the doctor and I guess the axle broke going down the Shaw Ranch field. I had no brakes, nothing. And the road was curve-y. I remembered Chalky Point [down near Stage Road by Mattei's], and I thought, 'How am I ever going to get around that?' We were just flying, coasting, and all of a sudden I went over a ditch and somehow the car stopped. Aunt Grace got out and she sat by the side of the road while I walked clear over to the halfway place where the men were threshing grain to get my brother to take her on to the doctor.

"I was working at her house, cooking for the threshers—about 8, 9 men, you know—on a wood stove…we did have electricity then but you couldn't pay the electric bill [chuckles] it was so high. We couldn't afford to use much electricity.

This grammar school photo was taken a few years before the "ditch day" high school escapade Elaine describes in her narrative. She is fourth from the right in the middle row. In the same row, the second girl from the right is Elizabeth Morimoto, one of the friends Elaine made in school and kept for life. To this day they still regularly correspond.

The faces in this photo clearly show the wonderful mix of ethnic backgrounds in Pescadero in the '20s and '30s: Italian; Irish; English; Portuguese; Japanese.

This page, left: *Elaine Shaw, about age 20.*

Opposite page, top: *Eating watermelon, left to right are Aunt Grace Shaw; Aunt Annie [Shaw] Adair; Elaine Shaw; Betty Gordon; Carol Shaw; Ruth Mary Shaw; Uncle Edgar Shaw. In the back is John Shaw. 1927.*
Lower: *Still eating watermelon 15 years later, left to right: John Shaw Jr.; Ruth, Carol and Elaine Shaw Steele at a Steele Ranch picnic. 1942.*

"We had outdoor plumbing. We did get electricity in 1931—or 1930, I guess it was—but before that we had Delco. The barns and the houses were all wired for this Delco. It was a little motor that generated the electricity some way. They had milking machines at one time; but they didn't work out. The Delco ran the cream separator and the lights, just for the house."

COURTSHIP AND MARRIAGE [1936]

Three years passed before her Uncle Charlie offered Elaine an opportunity to attend the university at San Francisco. But then romance unexpectedly intervened. On August 7, 1936, she married Stanley Steele of the well-known Coast dairy farm family. Having once courted her older sister Carol, Stanley Steele was no stranger; Elaine had known of him, and his family, all her life.

"Well, our families, the Steeles and the Shaws, were old friends. In fact, my Uncle Edgar—the bachelor uncle—was engaged at one time to Clara Steele, my husband's aunt. But Edgar couldn't leave the ranch or his mother, and [my] Aunt Grace was kind of sickly; poor Clara Steele had her mother and kind of a sickly sister, too. They broke up; then [Clara] and her sister [Emma] both died in the 1920 flu.

"So, to tell you how I met my husband, Stanley. He went through high school before my brother and sisters got there, because he was a little older, but I always knew of him. When he was 18, he liked my older sister, Carol. He lived down the Coast, but he used to come to see Carol up at the ranch. She was 16 when he used to take her to the dances; I was only 12 and he was nine years older.

"Carol and Stanley sometimes would sit and hold hands and Ruth and I would get hysterical, or I guess we got naughty, so my father would send us to the bedroom.

"In those days they had Soccer Balls and Carnelian Balls at the high school, you know high school dances. My sister Carol was in Santa Cruz then, staying with Aunt Bertha and Uncle Ben Blaisdell and helping out; I was still on the ranch. Carol came up in October, and she and I went to the Supper Ball. Stanley asked me to go to supper. That's what happened."

"[Carol] was going with Norman Steele...and after that, with her future husband from Santa Cruz. I'd been out of high school three years; I wanted to go [on] to school, but couldn't. My father died when I was 15 and so I had to go down to help Aunt Grace. I didn't know how to cook. Aunt Grace taught me some, because I had to cook for her and Uncle Edgar and Frank George, the hired man.

"Then in 1935 my Uncle Edgar and Uncle James in San Francisco both died. They were guardians for

Carol, Ruth and I—John was old enough at 21, I guess, when Dad died. My other uncle in San Francisco, Charlie, knew I wanted to go to school to be a teacher. Somehow he got me to the state college in San Francisco. I started in January but in March [Stanley] gave me a ring. I really can't remember [how he proposed]. Isn't that awful? I know he came with a ring. It wasn't a very big stone, but it was 1936. It was all he could afford, I guess.

"We got married in August. I was always sorry I never finished [school], but we were all sort of uprooted; we had no home, in a way. Everybody helped us. We were very fortunate in that way."

The couple moved down to Chalk Ridge Orchard, Stanley's family place at Año Nuevo, to live with his parents and Stanley's orphaned nephew. Stanley split his time between working the Shaw Ranch and at Chalk Ridge, and the couple raised their two girls, Ruth and Sandra Steele. But that's another story [see page 131].

The Shaw Family 103

Girls and John Shaw Sr. enjoy a hay ride on the Shaw Ranch while the men are threshing. 1908.

Sources

All photographs are from the John Elias Shaw and Elaine Shaw Steele Collections archived in the Pescadero Historical Society inventory unless otherwise noted.

Alexander, Philip W. — *History of San Mateo County*. Press of Burlingame Publishing Co.; Burlingame, CA. 1916.

History of San Mateo County, California; Vols. I and II (Biographical) Illustrated. By Roy Walter McCloud; the S.J. Clarke Publishing Company; Chicago, Illinois. 1928.

Marschner, Janice — *California 1850 — A Snapshot in Time*. Coleman Ranch Press; Sacramento, CA. February 2000.

Interview with Elaine Steele, Scotts Valley. Pescadero Historical Society, July 29, 2003; informal interviews conducted over 3-year period with both Mrs. Steele and her daughter, Mrs. Ruth Moore.

Lague, Jim for Yuba Feather Historical Association — *History of Butte County, Vol. I* by Joseph F. McGie, 1982.

Mount Hope Cemetery list and *census records*

1920s' issues of *Pescadero Pebble* and *The Carnelian* and Pescadero High School yearbooks in school archives.

Shaw, Bertha — *Diary of Bertha Shaw, age 10. 1883-1884*. 66-127 Manuscripts, San Mateo History Museum Archives.

Shaw, Grace — *Grace Shaw Notes*. Pescadero Historical Society archives.

Shaw, John E. Jr. — *Shaw Genealogy*. (Donated by Ruth Moore, February 2004)

Sherow, Victoria — *Life During the Gold Rush*. Lucent Books; San Diego, CA. 1998.

Wikipedia and various online sources for histories of England, states, and counties.

Wilcox, Del — *Voyagers to California*. Sea Rock Press; Elk, CA. 1991.

The McCormick Family
Sister Marie Elise McCormick

Sister Marie Elise McCormick, "Sister Beth," at the Bútano family home of Joan McCormick. May 31, 2004.

Elizabeth ("Beth") Clare McCormick, born in 1919, is a third-generation member of the Irish Catholic McCormick family that has lived in Pescadero. After her father's early death, Beth was raised by her mother in the gracious 19th-century house on Old Stage Road that Beth's grandfather built. She went to school in Pescadero through the seventh grade and then moved to her mother's childhood home in Santa Clara where she attended St. Clare's School. There she made good friends with several of her teachers, but it was not until she was going to Notre Dame High School in San Jose that the first insistent thoughts of a spiritual calling entered her mind.

In the beginning Beth fought these inclinations and couldn't decide what to do. One day on her way to catch the streetcar that would take her from her school in San Jose back home to Santa Clara, she resolved to settle the matter by talking it over with Father Deesey at St. Joseph's Cathedral. He wasn't there, but other priests were and Beth thought it wouldn't hurt to say confession while she was at the church. She never mentioned the subject to the man behind the screen, but when he spontaneously asked her if she'd ever considered entering the convent she felt as if the Holy Spirit had spoken directly to her and she was at peace.

Beth entered the Sisters of Notre Dame de Namur as Sister Marie Elise McCormick on July 31st, 1937. With her deep love of books and learning driving an ambition to teach, she studied at the College of Notre Dame in Belmont and at Oakland's Holy Names College. In her long life as a professional educator she has taught in many schools all over the state of California, and one in Seattle, Washington. Known affectionately as "Sister Beth," she often visits the Bútano for holiday reunions and still actively serves on the staff at Notre Dame in its financial office, as a teacher and principal, and as an LVN in its Saratoga infirmary. To this day she carries the strength of her conviction as a gift to all the women she has taught over the years and to the succeeding generations of her family and friends in Pescadero.

The Pioneer Generation

JAMES McCORMICK SR. AND JOHN McCORMICK

James McCormick Sr. was born in Dublin, Ireland in 1841, the son of Peter McCormick and Catherine Gibeny. The family immigrated to the United States in 1848 at the height of the Irish potato famine when James was 7 years old. We don't have records on how many children were raised in the Peter McCormick family, but since we do know that two of James's siblings—sister Kate, born in 1832, and brother John, born in 1838—lived in Pescadero at the same time as James we assume that they crossed the Atlantic, and later, came to California, together. The McCormicks settled in Carthage, New York.

By combining family memory with other historical accounts the story of how the McCormicks got to Pescadero goes like this: James McCormick, Sr., accompanied by his older brother John and his wife of two years, Mary Eliza Brownell, and sister Kate, boarded a boat in 1863 along with 600 others who wanted to escape from the Civil War. They sailed to the Isthmus of Panama, then crossed the narrow strip of land on "the dinky railroad then in service there," and picked up another boat heading north. They sailed into San Francisco harbor on January 15, 1864.

Not finished with boats, they all embarked again and went down to Santa Cruz to stay for nine months. When they got there, John was too ill to work; his wife Mary took a job working in a hotel to support them until John could get back on his feet. By that time, the McCormicks had decided to move to Pescadero, where both John and James found their first employment on dairy farms working as milkers and all-around-laborers. Their paths took different turns after that.

The patriarch of the present-generation Pescadero McCormicks, James McCormick Sr., pictured here on the upstairs veranda of the McCormick store. Ca. 1912.

In 1865 John and Mary and their son Joseph moved to the old Tom Moore Ranch and worked there for about a year. Then they went to the Souza Ranch on the San Gregorio Creek. During their two-year stint at Souza's, their daughter, Mary Janett McCormick, was born on April 22, 1865. Still strongly affected by events taking place on the East Coast, Mary's mother was wearing black in honor of President Lincoln's death, which had occurred the week before.

106 Portraits of Pescadero

The McCormick Family

I. **James McCormick, Sr.** [1841 Dublin, Ireland – 1919] and **Julia Ann Sheffrey** [1843 – 1875].
    II. Alice A. McCormick (1866 – 1963) married George Faulkenstein
        III. Alice and Jimmy
    II. Frances "Fanny" McCormick (1868 – 1951) married George H. Cushing; widowed. Married **Anthony "Tony" Enos** in 1920.
        III. Julia ("Jule") [January 1901 – 196?]
        III. Emma [March 1902 – October 21, 1977]
    II. Ella M. McCormick [1869 – ?] married William Murphy.
    II. Florence McCormick [1871 – ?] married Charles Bradley.
    II. **James McCormick, Jr.** [1873 Willowside Farm – 1923] and **Mary Elizabeth Graham** [1874 Santa Clara – 1949 Santa Clara]
        III. **James Graham ("Graham") McCormick, Sr.** [1909 – 2000 Los Gatos] and **Elinor Anne Martin** [1911 San Francisco – 1986 San Mateo]
            IV. **T. Martin McCormick** [June 28, 1939 in San Francisco]
            IV. Anne Mary McCormick (Montalvan) [June 28, 1942]
            IV. Joan Elise McCormick [November 25, 1943]
            IV. James Graham McCormick, Jr. [May 6, 1948 – March 8, 1998]
            IV. Elinor Mary McCormick (November 22, 1951)
        III. Catherine Mercedes McCormick [1910 – 1987] married Paul P. Targhetta [1911 – 1995]
        III. Patricia Ann McCormick (1912 – 2001) married Philip F. Dougherty in 1943.
            IV. **Mary Pat Dougherty (Kanzaki)** (Two children: **Steven John Bond** and Kelly Ann Bond)
            IV. John Philip "Jack" Dougherty
        III. Richard Anthony McCormick [1913? San Francisco – ?] and Jean
            IV. Michael; Kathleen; Mary Graham; Mark
        III. **Elizabeth Clare McCormick — "Sister Beth," Sister Marie Elise McCormick** [September 3, 1919 San Francisco]
    II. Lillian E. McCormick [1874; married George Winkle]; 2 children)
    II. **Julia ("Jewel") McCormick** [April 17, 1875 – ?]

The McCormick Family

I. **Kate McCormick** (born 1832; died in Pescadero, Dec. 8, 1908)
I. **John McCormick** [1838 Ireland – 1919] and **Mary Eliza Brownell** [1836 New York – 1928].
  II. Joseph W. McCormick [November 6, 1862 – December 15, 1866]
  II. **Mary Janett McCormick** [April 22, 1865 on Souza Ranch, San Gregorio Creek – ?] Married **Joseph Vicorino Azevedo** [Azores 1867, lived in Half Moon Bay] in 1893.
  II. **John Andrew McCormick** [May 14, 1868 – Dec. 27, 1937]. Married Carrie Belle Johnson [Jan. 23, 1876 – Feb. 28, 1950]; they had 12 children.
  II. Jennie Rosita McCormick [1869 – June 26, 1925]
  II. **Lizzie Ann McCormick** [November 7, 1871 – ?]. Married **Herman Frey** [1886 in Lobitas – 1940]. They had 7 children.
  II. Fred Eugene McCormick [February 14, 1874 – November 7, 1875]
  II. Frank Charles McCormick [April 1, 1877 – ?]
  II. James Henry McCormick, [June 4, 1879 – November 18, 1903].
  II. Arthur Omer McCormick, [September 9, 1881 – 1953] and Theresa McCormick [1888 – 1938].
    III. Henry McCormick [ca. 1904 – ?]
    III. Louis McCormick [ca. 1904 – ?]
    III. Violet McCormick [1906 – 1913]
    III. Mary Jane McCormick [1912 – 1938]

The family returned to the Tom Moore Ranch for two more years while John built up his savings. In 1870 he bought his own ranch on the Pomponio Creek and farmed it for 14 years before moving to Pescadero.

In 1884 John McCormick bought and moved everyone in his family except his wife into the Pescadero Hotel, at that time one of only two in town. In an interview done many years later, his daughter, Mary Janett Azevedo, remembers that the Pescadero Hotel seemed to bring bad luck.

Was the hotel haunted? A string of unfortunate incidents befell several people associated with it. When Mary's father first bought the hotel her mother refused to live in town for some time. When she finally acquiesced, she suffered from a persistent illness. The man who managed the hotel before the McCormicks was named McKenzie; his child drowned in the Bútano Falls. Then a scandal occurred when the daughter of one of the managers fooled around with the wrong person and caused a divorce; when the hotel was bought later on in the 1930s by an Italian man, he quarreled with his wife and "pushed" her down the stairs, consequently killing her. The hotel fell into disuse not long after.

But during the time John McCormick ran the Pescadero Hotel he enjoyed a brisk business. When tourists came down from San Francisco to holiday in the country, Martin McCormick says that the

hotel staff would take a buckboard up to the Tunitas (Ocean Shore) train terminal to meet them and bring them on down to Pescadero. The guests would stay at either the Pescadero Hotel or the Swanton House and were entertained at the Elkhorn Saloon, which at different times was also owned by the McCormicks. If anyone wanted to spend a couple of days in the redwoods fishing, they'd take them—again by buckboard—to one of the camps up Pescadero Creek. The premier camp was called Saints' Rest (Memorial Park). The facilities were simple, tents or cabins, but perfectly fine for a short stay. They would also ferry folks and picnic baskets out to Pebble Beach to enjoy the salt air and be dazzled by the semi-precious stones shining among the rocks.

Top: *John McCormick's spread at Pomponio Creek, taken from a lithograph in Moore & DePue's* Illustrated History of San Mateo County, *1878.*
Above: *James McCormick's elegant house, built in 1873, with his sister, Kate, on the front porch.*

The McCormick Family   109

A "SECOND YOSEMITE"

Meanwhile James McCormick too had moved on from work as a dairyman. He married Julia Ann Sheffrey, on January 12, 1866, bought land in the Bútano Canyon for its peacefulness and its timber, built an elegant white house in "downtown" Pescadero, and fathered seven children—six girls and one boy—all born in rapid succession. (He probably would have had more but his wife, Julia, died in 1875 at the age of 32 giving birth to their last baby, Julia, and James never re-married.)

In 1872 James went back to work at dairying and farming with two brothers newly arrived from France named Fernand and Joseph Levy, who had started a general store in Spanishtown [Half Moon Bay]. James liked the Levys but he quit dairying a year later to go into the business for himself when he bought into the Pescadero General Store from John Garretson. With his partner P.G. Stryker, James owned the business for four years before selling the store back to Garretson. This was probably due to the fact that during his tenure at the General Store, his personal attention was divided between the store's concerns and his civic duties as a deputy assessor and road supervisor for the town of Pescadero.

But his connections with the Levys remained unbroken. June Morrall reports in her 1978 book *Half Moon Bay Memories* that the Levys had been engaged in many enterprises reaching far beyond the scope of selling goods in their original Spanishtown store. They had a lumber business, for instance, with a 25-man crew that worked a mill near the Bútano Creek. In the '70s they opened a second store in San Gregorio, right next door to a popular saloon on the Stage Road; in 1883 they opened a third in Pescadero. Joe Levy ran this outfit and initiated home delivery by riding horseback from cabin to cabin, dispensing goods that he'd

Below: *The Levy Brothers' store occupied a former mercantile space run by earlier Pescadero pioneers. It was the center of town where the mail service, stagecoach lines, and Western Union offices were located. 1885.*

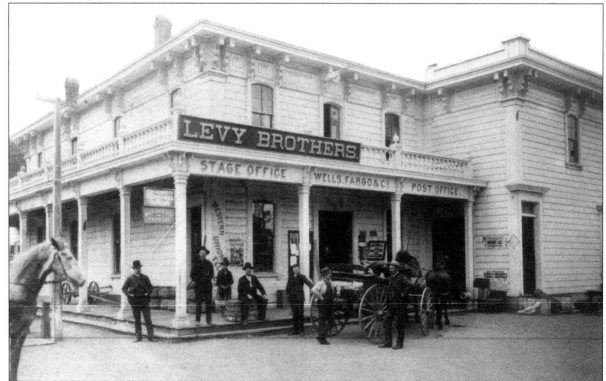

packed onto two mules that plodded patiently behind him. Joe carried on with this service until he sold the store to the McCormicks a while later [1884].

James McCormick's friendship with Joe Levy, and their shared interests, extended into the Levy logging enterprises in the Bútano Canyon, too. McCormick already had experience in the industry, having helped build some of the power mills in Santa Cruz, and he owned a part of the sawmill called Bútano Mill with Joseph Levy.

In the late '80s James was involved in the operation of his own lumber and shingle mill (Hamilton-McCormick Mill) as well, located on 24 acres of timberland that he had bought in the Canyon. His partner, Hamilton, was unfortunately killed early on in this operation when a stone flywheel disintegrated but James Jr. stepped in to work with his father.

Martin McCormick recalls that when they logged they did not go up very high, but stuck mostly in the flats of the canyon. They hauled the logs by oxen to the mill site and cut them down into standard lumber sizes. Then the lumber was hauled out to the coast and loaded onto tramp steamers bound for San Francisco and Santa Cruz. This went on until 1908 or '09.

James Sr. thought the Bútano was a wonderful place for people to buy lots for summer cabins. He subdivided his land into what he called the Bútano Falls Tract in 1912, composed of about 110 individual lots, each selling for between $200 and $800. In what Martin McCormick points out as an example of "Irish Marketing," James Sr. capitalized on the Bútano's spectacular falls by calling his getaway, "A Second Yosemite."

After James Sr. died in 1919 the Bútano developed into an enclave of well-off people looking for summer homes in the 1930s, '40s and '50s; in the '60s people started buying the cabins as permanent year-round residences and today roughly half of the Bútano is occupied by a resident com-

"Aunt Fannie," James McCormick Sr.'s second child, born in 1868, as a young woman. Ca. 1888.

With her first husband, George Cushing, she had two daughters, Julia and Emma. Fannie served two terms as Pescadero's postmistress, from 1894–1899 and 1934–1935; and ran the telephone office at the McCormick & Son building from 1903–1933. At age 52 she married Tony Enos after George died in an accident. For many years Fannie was also the town librarian.

Grandpa James McCormick with some of his grandchildren (left to right, Emma [seated]; Jule; James Sr. with Jimmy; Alice; Graham) in the gardens of the old Swanton Hotel's cottages in Pescadero. 1909.

The McCormick Family

Timeline 1900 – 1930
Highlighted parallel events in San Francisco Bay Area, California, and the Nation

1900 California State Automobile Association founded in San Francisco.
   Wave of Japanese immigration begins at turn of the century and continues through 1910.

1901 Republican Theodore Roosevelt is sworn in on September 14 after President William McKinley is assassinated.

1904 Theodore Roosevelt is elected President of the United States.

1905 War between Japan and Russia; Japan's victory thrusts the formerly isolated country onto the world stage as a major player.
   Industrial Workers of the World born in Chicago; the biggest marketing co-op in the state, the California Fruit Growers Exchange, is founded.
   The Ocean Shore Railway company is incorporated.

1906 San Francisco Japanese are ordered out of public schools and restricted to "Oriental" schools.
   On April 18 San Francisco is struck by a major earthquake and nearly destroyed by ensuing fires.

1908 Pres. Theodore Roosevelt's Gentlemen's Agreement stops the flow of Japanese workers into America.
   In the national November elections Republican William Taft wins the presidency.
   Henry Ford invents the Model T automobile.

1909 The first road-building bond is

DECORATED AUTOMOBILE "FLOATS" HIGHLIGHT A PARADE IN PESCADERO.

passed in California in the amount of $18 million. By 1910 there are 36,000 autos driving in California.

1911 California gives the vote to women, nine years before national suffrage is legislated.

1913 Democrat Pres. Woodrow Wilson is inaugurated on March 4.
   The Alien Land Law (Webb-Hartley Law) prohibits aliens ineligible for citizenship from buying farmland in California.
   California conservation commission formed to preserve and protect water; the Sierra Club loses their battle to save the Hetch Hetchy.

1915 The Victrola phonograph is invented.

1916 Woodrow Wilson is re-elected President.
   Electric clocks are introduced; there are 3.6 million cars in the United State, average price, $600.

Norman Rockwell creates the first cover illustration for "The Saturday Evening Post."

1917 The Russian Revolution overthrows the Czar and institutes a Communist state. On April 4 the United States, under President Wilson, enters World War I.

1918–1919 The great "Spanish flu" epidemic kills 50 million people worldwide and affects millions more.

1919 The 18th Amendment is ratified, inaugurating the "Prohibition" period (1920–1933).
   California passes a gasoline tax to pay for further road construction.

1920 The 19th Amendment is ratified and American women go to the polls to vote for the first time.
   Radio is the most rapidly growing medium in the '20s; the railroad industry peaks in importance as the

112 Portraits of Pescadero

munity. Everyone in the McCormick family—from James Sr.'s generation to the present—remembers the relaxed, happy times they spent in the Canyon.

James Sr.'s bright and entrepreneurial spirit made him a stand-out in the Pescadero community for over 30 years. Besides his lands in the Bútano, he owned significant pieces of property in Pescadero town itself, consisting of two lots, 200 x 300 feet, and 200 feet square on the main streets; and three acres in back of the Swanton Hotel. A Democrat, he served as deputy assessor and road supervisor for the town; he was closely connected with the Pescadero Fast Freight Company for three decades and at one time was its proprietor; and as an agent for the Pacific States Telephone Company he helped to bring in the telephone line to Pescadero.

James McCormick lived about six months longer than his brother, John. They both passed away in 1919 at the close of a decade that had seen the first great world war; the decimation of millions of people in the Spanish flu pandemic; suffrage for women in the state of California; and the births of many of their own grandchildren. These Irish men had escaped from famine in their native land, sought refuge from the terrible conflict of the Civil War in their adopted one, and left a legacy in a small American place that would endure for generations to come.

> *"While growing up in Pescadero as a child and teenager, James didn't have much in common with his siblings, the fact that they were all girls. When James was not working in his father's general store, McCormick & Son, he could be found ocean fishing at the nearby beaches. He loved going to the ocean and relaxing by himself."*
>
> — Steve Bond

JAMES MCCORMICK JR.

James McCormick Jr. was the fifth of James McCormick Sr. and Julia Ann Sheffrey's seven children. He was the only boy. Born on September 15, 1872 on his Uncle John's Pomponio farm at Willowside, he was sandwiched in between Alice, Frances ("Fannie"), Ella and Florence on one side and Lillian and Julia (also called Jewel), on the other. In the same year that the last girl, Jewel, was born, their mother died.

Being the only son, James Jr. worked closely with his father in his logging business and then in the family's general store,

---

automobile gains ascendancy.

California farmers begin bringing in Filipino laborers, raising the state's Filipino population of 3,300 in 1920 to 30,000 by 1930.

PG&E dominates power utilities in Central and Northern California.

1921 Republican Warren G. Harding is inaugurated in March.

Edith Wharton wins the Pulitzer Prize for her novel "The Age of Innocence."

1923 President Harding dies in August; Vice President Calvin Coolidge takes office and is re-elected the following year. In December he initiates the first radio broadcast of a Presidential address.

1924 Congress passes the Oriental Exclusion Act, prohibiting all immigration of Japanese citizens.

1925 The "Scopes Monkey Trial" takes place in Dayton, Tennessee.

1926 The first talking motion picture "Don Juan" is shown to a public audience in New York City.

1927 Charles Lindbergh makes his famous transatlantic solo flight in the "Spirit of St. Louis."

1928 Republican Herbert Hoover is elected President.

1929 On October 24, "Black Thursday," the New York Stock Exchange crashes with $4 billion lost in trading, ending the prosperity that followed World War I.

Top left and right: *When "Jewel" McCormick (left) introduced her girlhood friend Mary Elizabeth Graham to her brother James, their chemistry was irresistable.*

Opposite page, top: *They married in 1908. Mary, 34, and James, 35, made a true love match.*

McCormick & Son. James Jr. liked to design and build homes and was an accomplished carpenter. As he was very well liked, too, his business did well. He built several homes in the Pescadero area, including one for the McCormick clan up in the Bútano.

James entered his thirties soon after the century clicked over into a new epoch. His sister Julia introduced him to a close friend of hers from Santa Clara. Mary Elizabeth Graham was physically beautiful and—even better—she had a beautiful spirit. She seemed to give herself completely to life—you could hear it in her laugh—and she was nobody's fool. This turned out to be a true love match. James and Mary were married on May 5, 1908.

The McCormick store was the center of their lives. James Jr. worked there with his cousin John during these years, and the first four of his children were born in the bedroom upstairs. James and Mary had their first child, James Graham on February 25, 1909. For a while it looked as though

Left: *Hunters gather in front of the McCormick store in the 1910s. From left to right they are Charlie Steele, (Arthur) Pat McCormick and Alex Moore (Clifford Moore's father). The "Bell" sign indicates that the telephone office was up and running at this time.*

Opposite page, clockwise from left: *"Washing done while you wait in Pescadero," by Patricia Ann and Sis; Patricia Ann, Catherine, and Graham; Patricia Ann; Mary McCormick with Catherine, Graham and Patricia Ann, 1912.*

114   Portraits of Pescadero

The McCormick Family

The McCormick house, early 1900s; James Jr. and Mary moved in about 1920. Inset below: Beth McCormick.

Graham, as they called him, would grow up in the same family pattern as his father, because three of his siblings were girls—Catherine, Patricia Ann, and Elizabeth Clare—but he was saved by his brother, Richard Anthony.

Steve Bond gives us an intimate glimpse of the McCormick household in a description of his grandmother, Patricia Ann, from his memoir, *The Evolution of my Family*.

"Patricia Ann was the most mischievous out of all her siblings. She was always getting into something or snooping where she wasn't supposed to. Her sense of adventure got her into trouble sometimes. But even as a child she had a keen sense of getting out of trouble and her great sense of humor helped her in these situations.

"My grandma was very active: she and her brothers and sisters played many games. The times she enjoyed the most were the ones when her parents would take all the kids out to the beach to go wading in the surf. She also enjoyed going to the movies on Saturday nights in the community center. The movies had no sound so my grandma's cousin, Louis McCormick, played the player piano throughout the whole movie.

"When my grandma was a teenager, she found going to the movies the fun thing to do, but then there were also the Pescadero High School dances. By far the most popular thing to do in Pescadero was to watch the soccer games between Pescadero High School and the other nearby high schools."

Across the street from the old Swanton House hotel, the family lived upstairs at the McCormick store until about a year after the fifth child, Elizabeth, was born in a hospital in San Francisco. Quarters were getting cramped, so after Grandpa James died they moved up the street to his house across from the Community Church.

116   Portraits of Pescadero

They were a happy, close family and Pescadero was such a lively, close-knit community in those days that it seemed everyone they knew were either cousins or almost like it.

This bright bubble burst in 1923 when 51-year-old James McCormick Jr. died from a perforated ulcer. There weren't any resident physicians in Pescadero at that time, and the nearest hospitals were as far away as Santa Cruz, San Francisco or over the hills in San Mateo. It took hours to carry him to an operating table and when the doctors performed surgery on him it was too late.

Three-year-old Beth was too young when he died to remember much about the kind of man her father was, but she recalled a poignant scene that occurred the day he was buried.

"I don't remember him. I'm sure he was a great man. They told me that when he'd come home from work, he'd lie down on a little couch we had. My mother would say, 'Go wake up your Dad' and I would go and give him a kiss and that would wake him up.

"[Then when he died] I remember ... exactly where the coffin was placed. And I remember my mother lifting me up to kiss him, which I did. They told me that I said to her, "Why doesn't he wake up?" Then I remember standing out on that porch upstairs in the bedroom that was right above that room, and watching the funeral procession going up the hill. The trees weren't covering it then, you could see the whole thing."

Mary McCormick came home that day and put away her grief in a private place. She had lost the love of her life, but, with five children to raise and educate and a household to run by herself, she had work to do.

MOTHER MARY MCCORMICK

Mary McCormick—or Mary G., as friends and family called her—got herself a job working as the janitor at the high school. At home she reorganized the family's private space so that she and the children could live comfortably on the second floor while downstairs the rooms were converted into quarters with separate entrances for boarders. The living room in front was shared at different times by two of the high school teachers, Miss Sheridan and Miss Schroeder; for a while Mr. White, the grammar school principal—"a very, very fine man"—slept in the back bedroom.

Everything functioned in a very compatible way. Sister Beth remembers, *"One night when Mr. White was there, our dog, Butano, came barking and barking and barking. Finally Mr. White got up and opened his door. The dog would run a little way, and come back. Finally he followed and found that the tank house was overflowing—all the water was coming down. The dog was gonna warn us. [laughs] I don't know how they fixed the tank house, but anyway the dog had alerted him to that."*

Mary G.'s first Christmas in Pescadero at the Swanton Hotel cottages; she is pregnant with her first child, Graham. 1908.

Top: *Graham and his brother Dick McCormick were regular customers at St. Anthony's. 1928.*
Above: *Dick and Beth McCormick lived across the street from Pescadero's Congregational Church. 1923.*

Mary G. kept a kitchen garden, where she grew rhubarb among other things. In the lot next to the house, where Jim McCormick used to have the second White Front Garage (Dodge), she grew artichokes that she sometimes sold for extra pocket money. Artichokes needed a lot of irrigation. In 1923 the creek ran dry for a while in Pescadero because Woodside was pumping everything at the headwaters for recreational uses. The farmers in Pescadero had to cut holes in the creek bed until there was just enough seepage to keep the plants alive, and, fortunately, before he passed away James McCormick and his horses had done this for their artichoke patch.

Beth McCormick recalls they had two pigs, Georgette and Chiffon, and several chickens. There was no refrigeration in the kitchen, so anything they wanted to keep cool was kept in a box on blocks of ice that were delivered to the house. Vegetables were stored in the cool, dry bottom room underneath the water tower.

All the McCormick kids did their best to help out. Mary G.'s oldest son Graham took over as the man in the family when he was only about 14 and he sometimes helped his mother at the school; Catherine and Patty pitched in too. Sister Beth remembers that her mother and sister Patty were great cooks: Mom often made a big pot of navy beans with ham—nothing fancy, but very satisfying—and Patty loved to make desserts. Sister Beth claims that since she was the "baby" of the family, she was spoiled—she came straight home from school but her chores usually didn't amount to much, just bringing in kindling wood for the kitchen stove, setting the table for dinner. She wasn't allowed to light the fire until everyone else got home.

The McCormicks were lifelong members of Pescadero's Catholic community and strong supporters of the faith. James McCormick Sr. had given the lumber from his own mill to build St. Anthony's some 55 years before. Mary McCormick taught catechism to the children there and prepared them for confirmation and first communion. The priest never lived in town—he came down one weekend a month from Half Moon Bay where the diocese headquarters for Pescadero was centered at Our Lady of the Pillar. Father McDaniels would arrive Saturday at the McCormick's, share their evening meal, and stay overnight. The next morning he'd say the Sunday mass and ride back to Half Moon Bay in the afternoon.

Two of Mary G.'s best friends were "Tot" Williamson [Louise Moore] and Doris Goulson Vierra; her oldest children were good

Top: *Starting in 1867 and finished in 1870, Saint Anthony's Catholic Church on North Street was built with lumber supplied by James McCormick, Sr.'s mills. The church bell tower was not added on until 1888.*

Above: *The first public grammar school, built in 1875, was right next door to St. Anthony's. Only one of the rooms in this beautiful two-story building designed by architect John McKay was used. Between 25 and 30 pupils attended.*

friends with Harriet and Earle Williamson. But Mary G. didn't have much time to spend with her friends. When she wasn't busy with her family and work, she was frequently called upon by other townspeople for her counsel or her help.

"My mother was a very wonderful woman. ... There was just something about her that when people were in trouble they would come to her. ... Most of the time I was growing up there was no doctor or dentist in Pescadero. We had to go to Half Moon Bay. But people used to come to my mother when they'd get sick or in trouble. She was really a very steady, strong, and loving person."

— Sister Beth

Mary G. was also a force to be reckoned with. No one would ever ask for her opinion if they couldn't stand hearing the truth, because the truth as she knew it was definitely going to be Mary G.'s response.

"We had a Judge Woodhams here in Pescadero, and Walter Moore was the sheriff. They were the only two people in Pescadero that had authority in any way—we never had a mayor. I remember one incident, my two sisters went to choir practice—neither one of them could sing, so I don't know why they did—at the church. We had a car called an Ajax [laughs]—I don't think they make 'em any more. They left it in front of the church, right in the road there in front of St. Anthony's in Pescadero and when they came out from practice their car was gone. There was an old wreck of a car in its place. So they went home and told my mother. She called Walter Moore. He came down and took a look at the car and he said, 'I know whose that is.' He drove to Half Moon Bay, where they were having a dance. Got these two fellers that he knew was their car and they'd had a little bit too much to drink. Anyway, he brought them

and the car back and he said to them, 'Now, shall I take you to Mary McCormick, or to Judge Woodhams?' And they said, 'Oh, Judge Woodhams, please!'"

Mary G. held it all together until her oldest children were well launched into the first phase of their young adulthood and continuing their education. As Graham and, later, Patty graduated from Pescadero Union High they went to live with their grandmother in Santa Clara; Graham attended the university there, and Patty went to San Jose State to become a teacher. Catherine had gone to live with Aunt Elizabeth Graham in San Francisco while she went to business school. Mary G. sold the McCormick house to the Swigerts in about 1930 and moved to a little house near the high school for another year until Dick graduated. Dick was destined for Santa Clara, too. With only Elizabeth left in the house, Mary G., now in her mid-fifties, left Pescadero and moved back to her childhood home.

These two photographs of the I.D.E.S. (Chamarita Festival of the Holy Ghost) celebration taken by Ravnos on May 31, 1914, give a good picture of Pescadero town prior to the 1920s.

On the opposite page the band is just passing the Commercial Hotel (formerly Swanton Hotel) and you can see the Emporium and Ocean Shore Market.

Above, the crowd is passing the Methodist Episcopal Church (now the Native Sons Community Hall), the I.O.O.F. hall, and the Woodhams' house, lured by the smoke rising from the I.D.E.S. barbecue grills at the end of the street.

Modes of transportation have overlapped throughout Pescadero's history. The Enos & Nunes stable, catering to horse-drawn carriages and stagecoaches common in past eras, was just as vital to keeping folks mobile in the 1920s as the White Front Garage that serviced the automobile.

The Roaring Twenties

SMUGGLERS AND FIRES

Beth's memories of Pescadero in the 1920s evoke a period of both high spirits and calamity that changed the course and character of the town's future. The series of fires that broke out in the '20s destroyed houses and public buildings and punched a serious hole in the town's economy, but Pescadero folks picked themselves up and rebuilt what they could. As ever in the town's history, family and community relationships were only strengthened by whatever adversities people faced together. When a crisis had passed, they went fishing or off to the beach for a picnic. Life and gossip continued to flow in and out of the stores as folks picked up their groceries; visited the garage, the saloon and the ice cream parlor; and attended school functions.

In other parts of the state and in the country, this was an intoxicating era of abandonment and inebriation. The Great War and the Spanish flu pandemic were gradually fading nightmares; and women in the whole nation joined their California sisters on November 2, 1920 to exercise their right to vote.

Everyone wanted to party. In the 1920s the coastline saw a lot of moonlight action with men in boats sneaking to and from the shore loaded with illegal contraband of alcoholic content. Año Nuevo was one such favorite off-loading site, but June Morrall tells a juicy story about a violent "whiskey war" closer to home in her book, *Half Moon Bay Memories: the Coastside's Colorful Past*.

Beth McCormick and cousin Gerry Graham loved to swim.

In December, 1924 a bunch of smugglers unloaded $20,000 worth of scotch whiskey on a beach near Pescadero and buried it for safe-keeping while they went back to get more. Unknown to them, five local residents hiding in the rocks saw them bury the cache. When the smugglers left, the five men went down to dig up the loot and quickly carried it off to town. We don't know if their intentions were honorable or not. They might have been thinking they would turn the stuff in to the constable, or, if keeping it for themselves, to use the whiskey purely for medicinal remedy. Whatever their plan was, when they got back to town they generously distributed the bottles among several households that were willing to safeguard them.

By the time the smugglers returned to the beach with a second load later that night, they got wise and stormed in high dudgeon to Pescadero. The smugglers rampaged through town brandishing weapons, roughing up innocent citizens and breaking into houses until they found one of the hijackers and tortured him into telling them where the whiskey was. Later, when all the shooting and shouting was over, townspeople found a [deserted] site where the smugglers had been operating in the hills east of town, including a large moonshine still.

Numerous fires that sequentially devastated over half of Pescadero during the '20s severely tested the town's economy. Why were there so many? For one thing, there was no organized fire depart-

Fourth of July celebration at the McCormicks' stronghold in the Bútano. The gentleman at the extreme left is James McCormick; the man at the far right is probably his brother John. No date.

---

ment in town and for another, during some of those years Pescadero Creek ran low or dry. And everything was made of wood; all it took to start a fire was an unattended spark.

The first major fire to affect the town happened in 1921 and an even worse one, the Big Fire of 1926, leveled the northwest side of San Gregorio Street (Stage Road). In her journal Grace Shaw recalls that on March 20, 1926, *"A terrible fire burned J.C. Williamson's new store, the Koster Shop, Mr. Gianola's Saloon, the old Montevaldo Building, old S____ and Native Sons use to meet up over the store. It started at the coast side first, [then] burnt Duarte's, the White Palace Market butcher shop, Reese Store, Mrs. Frances Enos' home where Mr. and Mrs. J.C. Coburn once lived. Carl Coburn once had his bakery shop and candy store where Reese Place was. The post office was in that building and Mr. Leighton was the postmaster."*

A little more than a year later, on April 21, 1927, the Lone Pine Inn (formerly the Swanton House) and some of its cottages burned to the ground. Pescadero oldtimer Noel Dias remembers that he helped to pull things out of the building. There were rumors circulating around that the fire may have been set by arson in order to collect the insurance money, but this is not substantiated.

Noel Dias says that in the mid-Twenties the Emporium store, the McCormick store, Goularte's blacksmith and butcher shop, and the phone office were all on Stage Road in the center of town. The Coastside Transportation Company also had a big building on the main street, occupied today by "Made in Pescadero." The Transportation building was the central pickup point for a collectively-run fleet of trucks that hauled artichokes grown by the local farmers up to the big market in San Francisco. The Big Fire started when a guy went in to check the gas at the Coastside Transportation Company. He lit a match and the place blew up. Fortunately the man escaped with his life, but the town didn't fare so well.

Noel goes on to say that when he was in high school fires in the area were so common the school principal had procedures down to a drill. He'd take

Above left: *Both Dick and Graham McCormick (with fish) were accomplished fishermen from boyhood.* Above right: *McCormick clan women enjoying a picnic in the Bútano.*

the high school kids out of class and up to the "third falls" and they'd walk the trails to keep the fire from jumping. He remembers the smoke coming in "like fog." After he graduated there was a big fire at Crown 9.

Grace Shaw remembers that one, too. On November 21, 1929, she writes that there was a bad fire up on Pescadero Creek. *"Edgar and John got their new tractor this p.m. John had to use it, as the fire came over our hill, Shaw Bros. Ranch—back of Brother John's house by the pine tree. We were so frightened—it burnt about 60 acres on the Shaw Ranch. The girls were so frightened and afraid—stayed down at the house with me that night. Lizzie and Bernard [Cabral] came up and I rode up on the Chandler Road to see the fire. It was on "Billie Bins," now the Lane Ranch [Crown 9]."*

Beth McCormick was too small to help out when the Big Fire of 1926 occurred, but her mother was one of the many townspeople who immediately grabbed a bucket and ran to the town's defense.

"We had a lot of fires in Pescadero. People would just have to go out with buckets of water because we did not have a fire department. I remember one occasion when my grandmother and her sister from Santa Clara were visiting with us. It was a big fire—it was a store that was burning. My mother left me with my grandmother and went to help out. As she was going through a door [of the store] these two boys were carrying something very heavy, and they said, "Get out of our way!" and she stepped aside. Here was my brother, Dick, and his friend carrying a whole box of dynamite out of the store! They were going to take it down to the beach and I don't know what they were going to do with it, throw it in the ocean, but they were going to get it away so it wouldn't explode. And here they were, carrying it. She didn't even know Dick went to the fire. He must have been only in grammar school at that point.

"Everybody would join in. That's when the Japanese would come and help us. They were very nice people—I was very fond of them. The Japanese would always come up if they heard about a fire, bring their buckets and their hoses, get water and try to help put it out and then they would disappear back to their homes."

Another factor that contributed to fires getting out of control was that Pescadero had no telephone system installed yet and news could not travel fast enough to the outlying areas for anybody to respond quickly to town emergencies.

"One time, coming down from the Bútano to go to mass on Sunday morning, we found out that my Aunt Frances [Enos]—Aunt Fannie, we called her—her whole house was completely burned down. [The house was situated in the present-day Duarte's parking lot.] There wasn't any communication system really and as it burned during the night we didn't even know it."

DANCING ON THE BOYS' TOES

Beth learned to read before she started school, and books became a lifelong passion. Her mother always encouraged her young daughter's developing mind.

"I'll tell you how I learned to read. When we'd go to bed at night, my mother was a great one for reading in bed. She'd have the paper or whatever, especially on Sunday. I used to like the funnies—in those days the funnies were funny, like the 'Katzenjammer Kids'—she would read me the funnies and I would watch the pictures as she read it. Then she'd give it to me and she'd go on to her book. I'd take the paper and try to read it all over. I connected the picture with the words. If I came to a word I didn't know, I'd ask, 'What's this word?' and she'd tell me again. I don't know how she ever got through her own reading."

As she became an adept reader, Beth haunted the town library in the McCormick building, run by her Aunt Fanny, poring through every book. She went to the Pescadero elementary school from the first through the fifth grades.

"In the first and second grades I had Miss Layton; in the third and fourth grades, Miss Pinkham. In the fifth grade, I had Miss Pitcher who was from Half Moon Bay. We weren't too fond of Miss Pitcher because she always rooted for Half Moon Bay when Pescadero played against them, so that was a black mark against her. Then in the sixth and seventh I had Mr. Lewis."

In 1924 all the kids moved to the I.D.E.S. Hall where classes were taught while a new elementary school was being built. When the school opened, Beth went there for two more years and finished seventh grade.

Noel Dias and Sister Beth remember that at the Pescadero Union High School the kids learned chemistry; English; home cooking; Spanish; bookkeeping; and mechanical drawing in the six classrooms arranged around a central "rec" room inside the building. This spacious room was used as a community center for many pur-

An Engagement Announcement dated June 19, 1923 shows a gathering of local women in the Bútano. In the back row some of the names listed are Margaret Dias; Aunt Fannie; Ruth Coburn; —; Florence. In front are Jule; Louise Williamson with her baby, Harriet (?); Emma, and Beth McCormick.

poses: it had a stage and could be used for meetings; kids played basketball and other active games.

Sister Beth remembers: *"We used to have movies there, too. The movies were all black and white, no sound. The little kids would sit up in front, some on the floor, and someone would read the script that was on the film out loud. Then they would take all the chairs away and put them on the side; the high school kids and the adults would dance and the young kids would run in between. Nobody seemed to get in anybody's way. It was a lot of fun."*

Meanwhile, since Beth was only a young girl, her main point of business was to enjoy herself. She always went right home after school and after doing a few chores, she'd go out to play.

"My friend Billy Swigert, who was right across the street, would come over and we would play, [laughs] climb trees. The creek was very available to us—it went all the way around the house—and there weren't many trees or much brush around it then so we could go right down to it. My brothers built a little rowboat and we'd take it out. We had a lot of fun in that creek."

One of her best friends was Olivia Arcangeli, whose father owned Arcangeli store. She also played with Sally and Jane Woodman, who lived up where Phipps' is now, and she remembers several Japanese friends—Toshiko Morimoto and Sumi Kato. Beth says they didn't see each other much outside of school, because when the regular school day was finished, the Japanese kids would have to go to their Japanese school and then all go home to where they lived down the coast.

"We also would have parties and picnics at the beaches. That was great. Every once in a while there would be a run of smelt in the ocean. Someone would say, 'The smelt are running!' There would be schools of them—I don't know if you know what smelt are, but they're good to eat. They're not very big fish. So people would grab their gunny sacks and go down to the ocean and wade in and just get sackfuls of smelt and put them up on the sand; then go back in and get another sack. They'd bring 'em up to town and everybody'd enjoy smelt for a few days. That was fun to do that."

Aunt Fanny's husband, Tony Enos, had his own method for catching fish. Graham's son, Martin McCormick remembers it well.

Saints' Rest was a favorite sanctuary in the redwood forest where the McCormicks took their friends, family and hotel guests to restore their spirits. This image is from a hand-colored photograph taken in the early 20th century.

"Tony Enos lived just a couple doors down the street here in town. He was a great surf fisherman. He would always plan a trip or two each summer while we were staying up in the Bútano to go surf fishing. He kept all these abalone guts in a mayonnaise jar and you wanted to be way back when he opened that jar. He used boulders and bags filled with sand for the weights. He had all these multiple hooks that he would put the abalone guts on. They worked! We used to catch capizon. We would go out by Franklin Point and the fishing was great."

On the Fourth of July, while the rest of Pescadero would be putting up red, white, and blue bunting and staging parades down Main Street, the McCormick family always went up to the Bútano to camp in tents or, later, stay at the cabin Beth's father had built. They went fishing for steelhead and jumped in the creek for a swim up near the big falls. They'd get happily sandy and muddy and then tramp back to enjoy meals cooked over a wood fire.

For the older kids and the grown-ups, there were plenty of opportunities to socialize, too. All anyone needed was an idea and folks would invent their own entertainment—make their own music, play cards and parlor games, improvise croquet and tennis courts—at any number of houses. The Williamsons' and McCormicks' both had big enough places in the Bútano where they could have dances and picnics.

Delight Durant [Castle]'s family had a place up in the Bútano, too. Although she was very young, she remembers all the excitement.

"That was the Roaring Twenties, and my older sisters really kicked up their heels. ... The cabin, all the furniture would be moved out of it. It was an old wood floor so they'd sprinkle talcum powder on it so they could really dance. My brother would generally wind up the phonograph and they'd dance to that until it was time for them to go to bed. The McCormick boy [Graham] dated my older sister, Lois, different times.

"Noel Dias and his older brother John would come. Noel was very quiet; John was a lot of fun and he was very outgoing. They'd let me dance on their feet, you know, make me think I was dancing. Standing on

For a short while the Pescadero Union High School classes met in temporary quarters while the new school on North Street was being built. Pictured is the "school bus." 1924.

their shoes. They were nice parties. There wasn't a lot of drinking, at least not in my presence. Maybe they went out in the woods and they drank, I don't know [laughs]. Anyway, they had a good time. Harriet [Williamson] would usually come and bring her saxophone. Anybody that had any talent, that person would always perform because we didn't have any other music."

Delight says that several other Pescadero people, like Tony Ines, played major parts of the canyon social scene. *"He had a cabin right across the road from us. That was the party place. In fact, I think my sister had her wedding breakfast there. They had outdoor tables and a big place to barbeque."*

Beth finished seventh grade the same year her brother Dick graduated from high school. It was an opportune time for her mother, Mary McCormick, to make the next big shift in her life. She moved with Beth and Dick back to her mother's place in Santa Clara. Beth went to eighth grade at St. Clare's and then on to Notre Dame High School in San Jose. At 17, she answered a spiritual calling and entered the Sisters of Notre Dame as Sister Marie Elise McCormick. Her own destiny was laid out before her in a clear path and she embarked on the fulfillment of her life's dream to become a teacher.

Left: *Beth McCormick, about 6, poses on the porch with Butano, the family dog.*

Above: *Mary G. stands proudly in front of her flower garden. Late 1920s.*

Above: *Graham McCormick with his new car. Late 1920s.*

May 31, 1915 at Pescadero, California (Ravnos photo). Local man Ed Weeks says that Decoration Day—now called Memorial Day—was when townspeople would go up to the cemetery to lay flowers on the graves of their friends and relatives who had passed away. Initially begun in the 1860s after the Civil War, Decoration Day was honored in small towns all over America and persisted well into the 20th century.

Debbie Bennett Collection.

Sources

All photographs are from the Patricia McCormick Dougherty Collection archived in the Pescadero Historical Society inventory unless otherwise noted.

Alexander, Philip W. — *History of San Mateo County*. Press of Burlingame Publishing Co., Burlingame, Calif. 1916.

Bond, Steve — *The Evolution of My Family*, January 9, 1995. [Steve is the son of Mary Pat Dougherty Kanzaki and the grandson of Patricia McCormick Dougherty.]

History of San Mateo County, California, Vols. I and II (Biographical) Illustrated. By Roy Walter McCloud; the S.J. Clarke Publishing Company; Chicago Illinois. 1928.

Interview with Delight Castle, at Rob and Cotton Skinner's barn, Pescadero, May 8, 2004. Pescadero Historical Society.

Interview with Noel Dias, at the barn on Pescadero Creek Road, September 19, 2003.

Interview with Sister Marie Elise McCormick, at her niece's home (Joan McCormick) in Bútano Canyon, May 31, 2004. Pescadero Historical Society.

Interview with Martin McCormick, Pescadero, California December 2, 2003, interviewed by Clinton Blount, Sandy Lydon, and Meg Delano.

Mount Hope Cemetery list

Morrall, June — *Half Moon Bay Memories: The Coastside's Colorful Past*. Moonbeam Press, El Granada, California 1978.

Shaw, Grace — *Grace Shaw Notes*. Pescadero Historical Society archives.

Stanger, Dr. F.M. — *An Interview with Mrs. Mary McCormick Azevedo of Half Moon Bay*, taken on 2/20/1957. From 64-87 Transcripts at the San Mateo History Museum Archives.

The Steele Family
Ruth Louise Steele

*Ruth Louise Steele (Moore), on the right, and her mother
Elaine Baldwin Shaw (Steele). Pescadero, 2005.*

*I*n the back of her home on North Street, scores of wild yellow finches dart in and out of leaf shadows as they chatter over hanging containers of seed in Ruth Moore's garden patio. Around the corner of the house, open to the fields, another small plot anchored by an old apple tree is full of healthy cucumbers, tomatoes, and squash. Here the master gardener trains her granddaughter, Katelyn Moore, in the fine art of growing things. Later, when everything has ripened, she will show her young apprentice, now six, how to pick, prepare, and serve them at the dinner table.

Ruth is carrying on the tradition she learned as a child from her grandfather, I.C. Steele, on Chalk Ridge Orchard farm in the old dairy lands south of Pescadero. Named after her two grandmothers (Ruth Baldwin Shaw and Louise Compton Steele), Ruth also carries tradition forward simply by being herself. She is a direct descendant of three family lines in Pescadero's genealogy — the large and complex Steele family; the Shaws; and the Goulsons — and is related directly or by marriage to many more, among them the Moores; Williamsons; and Vierras.

Ruth is a keeper of the stories and, if anyone, would seem to be the obvious choice for her generation's position as family historian. If she were to accept the title she wouldn't take on airs about it. Her interest in the genealogies of her own family and in local history have risen in a most natural way out of the experiences she remembers about her childhood, her family, the people she knows and has always known, and from having lived all her days in one place. Through the occasions and events of her life, whether they challenged or uplifted her, her philosophy can be expressed in what she says about her childhood: "I don't ever remember being unhappy. I think it was all good times. I don't remember any bad times. We really had a good life."

The Pioneer Generation

Top: *Louise Compton Steele (1873 – 1954)*.
Above: *The second Isaac Chapman (I.C.) Steele (1872 – 1973). Ca. 1894.*

FROM THE COLONIES TO CALIFORNIA

The Steeles that came to Pescadero in the 1860s hail from an early American colonial family that had its origins in Hartford, Connecticut and in Delhi, New York. Ruth Louise Steele (Moore)'s direct ancestry goes back to Nathaniel Steele III and his second wife, Dameras Johnson. Born on December 13, 1783 in Delhi, New York, Nathaniel was the sixth of nine children descended from English emigrants who had settled in the American colonies in the 17th century. By the time he was 24 Nathaniel had married, but his wife Ester died in 1815, a year after their fourth child was born. Nathaniel married Dameras about three years later and started a second family. Four of their five children—Frederick, Isaac Chapman, George, and Edgar Willis Steele—together with several of their first cousins—children of Nathaniel's brother John Steele and Polly St. John—were to play important roles in the development of both California's and Pescadero's agricultural history.

Nathaniel and Dameras's children were all born in Delhi, New York, a small, picturesque town that was the seat of Delaware County. In the days before the railroad rose to dominance, Nathaniel owned N. Steele & Co., a stagecoach and transport operation whose routes traversed the whole southeastern section of the state from the Catskills to Ithaca.

Nathaniel was smart, hard-working, and honest. He made a large fortune in his business, but lost it because of an unscrupulous "silent partner" who incurred some bad debts that Nathaniel was obliged to honor personally. Overwhelmed in the financial revolution that occurred after the suspension of the United States Bank in 1836, Nathaniel moved with his second family to Ohio, where his brother John Steele, wife Polly St. John, and their children had already set up a new household. Fifty-three-year-old Nathaniel cleared a half-acre of the "Western Reserve" himself, built a house and started farming, still not even dreaming about California.

Nathaniel and Dameras's oldest son, Frederick Steele, would be instrumental in the Steele family's future connection with the West Coast. In 1839, Frederick, 20, entered the Military Academy at West Point and began a distinguished 30-year career as an Army officer. In letters collected at Stanford University Libraries a century later, Fred's classmate and great friend Ulysses S. Grant recalls

The Steele Family

I. **NATHANIEL STEELE III** *m.* second wife **DAMERAS JOHNSON**.

  II. Frederick Steele [1819 New York – 1868 San Mateo]; Civil War and Mexican-American War veteran

  II. **ISAAC CHAPMAN STEELE** [1820 New York – 1903 California] *m.* **HULDA EMELINE STEELE**.

    III. **FREDERICK NATHANIEL STEELE,** [1846 Ohio – 1907 Green Oaks] *m.* **CHLOE WORDEN** [1848 Michigan – 1934 I.C. Steele Ranch]

      IV. **ISAAC CHAPMAN STEELE**, the second [1872 Green Oaks – 1973 Chalk Ridge Orchard] *m.* **LOUISE COMPTON** [1873 – 1954 I.C. Steele Ranch]

        V. Muriel Steele [1903 – 1934] *m.* **Harry A. Olund** [1902 Texas – 1938 Palo Alto]

          VI. Harry A. "Andy" Olund [1929]

        V. **STANLEY STEELE** [1907 – 1990] *m.* **ELAINE SHAW** [October 10, 1916]

          VI. **RUTH LOUISE STEELE** [4/ 8/1938] *m.* **CLIFFORD JAMES MOORE** [5/15/1933]

            VII. Marilyn Moore [January 16, 1958]

            VII. James Moore [March 21, 1960]

            VII. Barbara Moore [June 7, 1963]

          VI. Sandra Steele [October 21, 1940] *m.* Norman Gillette [March 5, 1937]

            VII. Douglas and David Gillette

      IV. Clara Steele [1875 – 1920]

      IV. Emma Steele [1880 – 1920] and twin brother, died at birth

      IV. William F. Steele [1883 – 1956] *m.* **Catherine Baumgarten** [1898 – 1989]

    III. Effie Steele [1850 Ohio – 1913 Año Nuevo] *m.* **Edwin Dickerman** [1845 – 1912]

    III. George Horace Steele [1860 Petaluma – 1913 Año Nuevo] *m.* Elizabeth Ann Chrisman [1869 Santa Clara – 1950 Año Nuevo]

  II. George Steele [1825 New York – 1901 San Luis Obispo]

  II. Edgar Willis Steele [1830 New York – 1896 San Luis Obispo]

  II. William Steele [1832 New York – 1854 Ohio]

The Steele Family

I. John Steele and **Polly St. John**

    II. Rensselaer Steele Sr. [1808 New York – 1886 California) *m.* **Clarissa "Clara" Jameson** [1824 Ohio – 1866]. Founded Cascade.

        III. Ebenezer Steele [Born in Ohio; died at age 16]

        III. Ella Adeliza Steele [1844 Ohio – 1919 White House Ranch] *m.* **Rutherford H. Brown** [1839 Louisiana – 1897 Willowside Ranch]. No children.

    II. [**Rensselaer Steele Sr.** *m.* second wife, **Hattie Younglove**]

        III. Rensselaer E. Steele Jr. [1869 Cascade – 1935 Cascade]. "One-Armed Steele" *m.* Gertrude Paulson but divorced. No children.

    II. Samuel Horace Steele [1810 New York – 1896] *m.* **Amanda M. Remington** [1826 – 1895]

        III. Omar N. Steele

        III. Samuel Bliss Steele [Born Ohio] *m.* Frances Elinora "Nonie" Crocker.

        III. John Steele

        III. Charles Edward Steele Sr. [1851 – 1930] *m.* **Ida Jane Moore** [1856 Pescadero – 1946]

            IV. Mae Chloe Steele [1880 – 1952] *m.* Elbert Russel Pinkham [1879 – 1955]

            IV. Norman Steele Sr. [1881 – 1959 Pescadero] *m.* **Fannie Braghetta** [1892 – 1973]

                V. Norman Steele Jr. [1910 – 1979]; Myrtle Steele [1912 – ?]; Tom Steele [1913 – 1993]

            IV. Grover Steele [1886 – 1961]

            IV. Charles E. Steele Jr. [1891 – 1976]

                V. Marion E. Steele [1925]

            IV. Perle Ella Steele [1893 – 1942] *m.* Ralph Raymond Woodman [1887 – 1952]

                V. Jane Marion Woodman [1918 – 1995]; Sally Woodman [1920]

    II. Nathaniel Steele [1812 – 1846]

    II. Mary B. Steele [1816 New York – 1884] *m.* cousin Osman N. Steele; widowed, she married **Seldon J. Finney** [1825 – 1875]. Two sons.

    II. Smith Steele

    II. JULIA ANN STEELE [no known dates] *m.* **WILLIAMS** [no first name]

        III. Harriet M. Williams [1827 – 1906] *m.* **Aaron Honsinger** [1824 – 1899]

            IV. Fred Honsinger [1853 – 1902]

            IV. Hattie J. Honsinger [1857 – 1917] *m.* **Josiah Caldwell Williamson** [1851 Massachusetts – 1899 Pescadero]

                V. Nellie Williamson [1881 – 1884] *m.* Gladys Williamson [1888 – 1924]

                V. Frank Grant Williamson [1885 – 1963] *m.* **Louise Alice Moore** [1892 – 1975]

                    VI. Earle Aaron Williamson [1911 – 1986] *m.* **Dorothy Mae Siegel** [1915]

                    VI. Harriet Helen Williamson [1894 – 1972] *m.* **John Dias** [1913 – ?]

                V. Florence Almira Williamson [1894 – 1972] *m.* **Walter Harold Moore** [1893 – 1977]

> **VI.** Walter Ellsworth Moore [1925 – 1999] *m.* Darline Rose Cabral [1925 – 1984]
> **VI.** Gordon Earle Moore [1919]
> **VI.** Francis Allen Moore [1933]
> **IV.** Jessie Honsinger [1861 – 1929] *m.* **Alfred James Goulson** [1860 Wisconsin – 1929]
> **V.** Douglas Carl Goulson [1893 – ?] *m.* Florence Lombard [1901 France]
> VI. Douglas Alfred Goulson [1922 – 1945] *m.* Virginia Theresa Shea.
> **V.** Doris Goulson [1898 – ?] *m.* Antone Vierra [1895 – 1958]
> **VI.** Evatt Douglas Vierra [1922] *m.* Barbara Felkins [1933]
> **VI.** Lois Joyce Vierra [1922] *m.* Houston Bernie Offill [1920 – 1993]
> **II. HULDA EMELINE STEELE** [1826 Ohio – 1896 Green Oaks] *m.* her cousin, the first **ISAAC CHAPMAN STEELE**. Refer to first page of family tree.
> **II.** John C. Steele

that he was "quick of repartee, a wiry, shrill-voiced wag whose friends could tell by an odd snapping of his eyelids when he was preparing to tell a joke."

Frederick graduated from West Point in 1843 as a commissioned officer. As the years went by, he went where the Army sent him; his achievements and devotion to duty were measured by his steady rise in rank. During the Mexican-American War he fought in territories that are now part of Mexico, and didn't really lay eyes on California until 1849. In that year he sailed around the Horn to serve on the staff of General Bennet Riley, the last military governor of California, at the San Francisco presidio. In his letters sent to his family he spun "glowing tales of the newest frontier." In 1854, while on leave in Ohio, he threw the lure out so temptingly the whole Steele clan was hooked. They made plans to follow their dashing kinsman out to the "Golden State" as soon as possible.

Cow Heaven

Frederick's brother, 30-year-old George Steele, and his older cousin, Rensselaer Steele, 47, were the first to come out from Ohio in 1855. Dazzled by stories of gold that had achieved the status of national folklore, the two headed straight for the foothill placer mines in Sonoma County. Their attempts to strike it rich quick failed, but George's youthful aspirations still soared somewhere in the stratosphere. While he stacked lumber for cash in San Francisco Rensselaer worked out a scheme. The cousins rented a farm near Petaluma and set it up as a base in anticipation of future Steele clan members' arrivals.

In 1856 George's brother Edgar Willis Steele followed, bringing Rensselaer's wife, Clara (Clarissa); their children Eben and Ella; and the brothers' parents, Nathaniel and Dameras Steele. The journey was eventful. The party sailed out of New York on the steamer *George Law* and arrived at the east port of the Isthmus of Panama safe enough, but while in transit over to the Pacific side by train, their progress was stalled by a civil riot. The train couldn't get around the disturbance and nothing could get through to it from the other side that could carry the passengers to their destination. The train was forced to go backwards. While crossing a bridge that spanned a deep, marshy stream, several of the cars derailed and plunged down a cliff. In the resulting pile-up, 200 people were killed

Frederick Steele was a 30-year veteran of the Union Army.

and many more were injured. Thankfully, the Steeles' car stayed on the track and they were not hurt. Finally rescued and delivered to the Pacific, they boarded another steamer. On the day they landed in San Francisco the party witnessed the hanging of criminals James Casey and Charles Cora by the Vigilance Committee before George and Rensselaer hustled them off to their new home at Two Rock Valley in Sonoma County.

Edgar found employment right away, cutting and binding oats at $2.50 an acre. It was rough work, as everything had to be done using a hand cradle, but 26-year-old Edgar was motivated. He made enough with his harvest money to lease some farmland and bought five cows at $75 (!) apiece. That first winter he put in 80 acres of potatoes and grain. A former teacher by profession, Edgar also started a singing school where he taught one day a week.

Meanwhile, by happy accident, Rensselaer's wife, Clara Steele, 32, gave birth to the California cheese industry. On her voyage to California she carried in her trunk an old, well-traveled cookbook that had belonged to her English grandmother. Hungry for the taste of cheddar cheese she remembered from her childhood days, Clarissa experimented with a recipe she found in the book. She "persuaded an Indian to rope and milk some of the wild Spanish cattle, and from the milk so obtained ... made some cheese." It proved to be excellent. The Steeles sent samples of Clara's cheddar with some of their farm produce to San Francisco. The cheese was an instant hit.

Nathaniel and Dameras's last remaining son, Isaac Chapman Steele, 37, "broken in health" and with only $1,500 to his name, arrived with his family on March 29, 1857. Isaac's apprehensions, if he had any due to his circumstances at the time, were immediately dissolved.

Folks in Sonoma County had thought the Steeles were crazy to attempt dairy farming in the California hills; according to local opinion, the

A young George Steele, inset above, and his ranch in San Luis Obispo County (top), in 1900. The ranch reflects the type of land sought by The Steele Brothers as they set up their California dairy empire.

country was only good enough to feed the few hardy Spanish cattle that had been left to run wild. Nevertheless, the Steeles had made significant headway at Two Rock Valley over the past two years. Their persistance proved to be prescient: the cool, foggy coastal climate kept the grass green and abundant most of the year, and renewed it soon after the summer's heat had dried the hillsides to hay. In all the years that followed, and in all the subsequent locations with similar conditions that the Steeles ranched, their animals survived several droughts that decimated drier areas of the state.

And Clara's cheddar was perfection. In spite of the widespread decline in the price of butter and cheese in the San Francisco markets, the Steele dairies' superior product had the public clamoring for more. With their success proven, the brothers—George, Isaac, and Edgar—and cousin Rensselaer felt confident to expand. Rancho Punta de los Reyes in neighboring Marin County, with its "abundance of rich bunch grass and clover and many springs of cold water," was a veritable "cow heaven." Under the name of The Steele Brothers, they struck an agreement with the landowner that allowed them to lease 15,000 acres with an option to buy, bought 155 cows, arranged for an exchange of the butter or cheese that they made for payment, and officially began operation of the first dairy in the San Francisco Bay area on July 4, 1857. The great Steele dairy industry was launched.

LOCATION, LOCATION, LOCATION

Over the next four years the Steeles built up the ranchland in Marin and increased their herds. By 1861 they had paid off their debts, owned 600 head of dairy cows, and had accumulated a surplus of $10,000 in cash. With everything going so smoothly, they were enthusiastic about finding still more pastureland.

At this time Loren Coburn, the San Francisco livery stable mogul, was serendipitously looking for grassland to give his horses' feet a rest, too. Coburn heard that a few miles south of the newly formed town of Pescadero Isaac Graham had pur-

Timeline 1930 – 1950
Highlighted parallel events in San Francisco Bay Area, California, and the Nation

MEMBERS OF THE GRANGE—MEN AND WOMEN—BOARD A TRAIN. BOTH ISAAC CHAPMAN STEELE (THE FIRST) AND OTHER MEMBERS OF THE STEELE COMMUNITY WERE INSTRUMENTAL IN FORMING AND MAINTAINING THIS IMPORTANT INSTITUTION DEVOTED TO THE BETTERMENT OF FARMERS IN THE PESCADERO AREA AND IN ALL OF CALIFORNIA.

1930 Construction of Oakland Bay Bridge starts; it is completed in 1936.
Between 1930-'32, 44 brief strikes take place in California.

1931 In September a bank panic spreads across the nation; over 800 banks are shut down in a month. By 1932 unemployment reaches 13,000,000.

1932 Franklin Delano Roosevelt is elected President of the United States. California at this time is overwhelmingly Democratic.
The Lindbergh kidnapping captivates the nation.

1933 The democratic Weimar Republic falls in Germany; Adolph Hitler rises to power and establishes himself as Führer. Stalin begins the great purge of the Communist Party in the USSR. They continue until 1939.

The New Deal restructures the monetary system and creates an array of federal agencies—such as the Civilian Conservation Corps and the Agricultural Adjustment Act—to regulate private industry and find jobs for millions in government-sponsored projects. In March the President's first Fireside Chat is broadcast on the radio.
Congress passes the National Industrial Recovery Act.
Prohibition is repealed as the 21st Amendment is passed.
Construction begins on Golden Gate Bridge in January; it is completed on May 27, 1937.

1934 In California 1,250,000 people are on relief, nearly 20% of total state population.
First water from Tuolumne River begins to fill up South San Francisco's reservoir at Crystal Springs Reservoir.

1935 Social Security Act is passed. Boulder Dam is dedicated on September 30.

1936 The Spanish Civil War is fought. Many Americans join the battle.

1938 The House Committee to Investigate Un-American Activities (HUAC) is created and begins serious investigations in 1941.

1939 World War II begins in Europe as Germany invades Poland and Great Britain and France declare war against Germany.
World's Fair in San Francisco on Treasure Island. Bay and Golden Gate bridges newly built.

1940 Germany, Japan, and Italy sign the Axis Pact in September. The Battle of Britain begins.
Franklin Delano Roosevelt is re-elected to an unprecedented third

term. Radios are in 30 million homes in America.

1941 Penicillin is mass-produced and plutonium is discovered.

On December 7, Pearl Harbor is attacked by Japanese. The Japanese are already in possession of Indochina and Singapore. On December 8, the United States declares war on Japan; on December 11, on Germany and Italy.

1942 April 1, 1942 the DeWitt Order outlines the evacuation of San Francisco Japanese.

Sugar, gasoline, and coffee are rationed and sales of new cars and trucks are banned. In the following year meat, fat, and cheese are rationed; shoes are limited to three pairs per person per year.

1945 G.I. Bill of Rights is passed.

President Roosevelt dies of cerebral hemorrhage. Vice President Harry Truman becomes President.

August 6, 1945 — Hiroshima, Japan is destroyed by the first atomic bomb used in a war. Japan surrenders on August 14.

Agriculture in California is a $2.5 billion-a-year business.

1947 In June the Marshall Plan outlining U.S. involvement in the reconstruction of Europe is introduced. A housing crisis becomes a major national concern in the U.S.

1949 Loyalty oath enforced by Regents of University of California at Berkeley campus, including regent Lawrence Mario Gianinni, President of the Bank of America.

1950 Agriculture in California is a nearly $3 billion-a-year business.

chased the enormous Rancho Punta del Año Nuevo—nearly 18,000 acres—for his winter cattle range but was letting it go due to personal and financial crises. Coburn promptly bought it on September 15, 1862. There were plenty of acres left over from his own needs to rent out to another enterprise, so at the same time Coburn made an arrangement with The Steele Brothers. Isaac Steele rented a horse from Coburn's stable and rode south to check into the possibilities. The Año land was another perfect "cow heaven."

Isaac leased the property from Coburn and his then-partner Jeremiah Clark for a period of ten years at the rate of $6,000 per year plus taxes. The deal included an option to buy 7,000 acres at $6 per acre—all of the Rancho south of the Gazos Creek—when the lease expired. The Steele Brothers formed a partnership with Horace Gushee and Charles H. Wilson (or Willison) and together made plans to develop their new holdings. They bought 1,100 milk cows at about $15 a head and brought them in from Marin by steamboat and barge and unloaded them at the mouth of the Gazos Gulch. They also brought in 13 Indian milkers from the Point Reyes dairy, but in 1864 the Indians went back to Marin County and Chinese workers from San Francisco took their place.

Isaac Steele built his New England-style home at Green Oaks Creek with lumber from nearby Waddell Mill; Rensselaer built a similar house on neighboring Cascade Creek. With thousands of acres to feed their happy cows, the Steeles sold cheese as fast as it could be made at 25 cents a pound. Their fortunes again soared.

Meanwhile the horrific Civil War was staggering on towards its conclusion in the eastern half of the continent. The Steeles' natural sympathies were Republican, allied with their old home in the North, and their close family connection with Major General Frederick Steele—who was deeply engaged in military actions on behalf of the federal government against the "Rebellion"—only strengthened their devotion to the Union cause. But being so far away from the center of the maelstrom, the California Steeles had to be creative in order to make a personal contribution.

They came up with a unique solution—a mammoth cheese! Workers collected 3-1/2 days' supply of milk—3,500 gallons—from 600 cows and, after making some adjustments to accommodate such a large quantity, applied Clara's recipe. They custom-built an outsized form to contain the giant cheddar while it cured. The finished cheese weighed in at 3,930 pounds, measured 20 feet in circumference, and was 18 inches thick. Such a thing had never been seen before; obviously it would require special handling to even lift

Cascade Ranch, from a lithograph in Moore & DePue's Illustrated History of San Mateo County, *1878.*

it, let alone transport it to another location, without breaking it into pieces.

The Steeles' inexhaustible ingenuity won out and this was accomplished. (The wood packing crate used for shipment was subsequently sawed in half and served for a quarter of a century as two picnic tables by Will and Catherine Steele.) The cheese was exhibited at the Mechanics' Fair in San Francisco in 1864 and sold to the public at $1 a pound, the proceeds going to the Sanitary Fund (the forerunner of the American Red Cross). Such was the novelty of the cheese that even after complimentary pieces of it had been cut and sent to President Lincoln, General Ulysses S. Grant, and General Frederick Steele, the Steeles' total donation to the Fund came to $2,820.

The Steele Brothers had established themselves as the biggest dairy operation in California. At Año alone they ran five dairies: Pocket Dairy at Pebble Beach Hill; White House Canyon, run by Horace Gushee; Green Oaks, run by Isaac Steele; Cascade, run by Rensselaer Steele; and Cloverdale, run by Edgar Steele. When their lease expired in 1872 the Steeles acted on their option to buy 7,000 acres from Clark and Coburn, who retained control of the Pocket and Cloverdale lands.

At this point, Edgar Steele had worked 16-hour days for eight years, milking 20 cows himself, handling general business matters at the dairy, and keeping the books for The Steele Brothers firm. Thoroughly drained, in 1864 he leased his dairies for a comfortable yearly income of over $5,000 and went back East for a long rest. He toured the Southern States for a couple of years after the War, and married a Tennessee general's daughter, Julia P. Stanley. When the Point Reyes lease expired his "holiday" was over. Edgar returned to California to look for new land for the Steele milk cows.

Circumstances were favorable. The drought of 1864 had destroyed entire herds of cattle in the southern counties and Central Coast ranchos were up for sale cheap. Edgar rode down to look at four of them in the San Luis Obispo area and saw that the country was as ideally suited to the Steeles' purposes as anything they had up north. He bought 48,000 acres at $1.10 an acre and The Steele Brothers immediately ante'd in. Edgar moved to San Luis Obispo with his wife to develop the newest (and what was to be the last) sector of the Steele Brothers' dairy empire.

Edgar's young wife Julia died in childbirth within a year, but he continued to live on at his home at the Corral de Piedra Rancho and plunged himself into public work. He helped set up the Bank of San Luis Obispo, serving as its president, as well as the San Luis Obispo Water Company. In the 1880s he was a Director of the Grangers' Business Association, a member of the Order of Patrons of Husbandry, and belonged to the International Order of Oddfellows. In 1876 he married again, this time to another well-bred young woman named Emma Smith, a teacher at Santa Barbara College. They had a son, Edgar J. Steele, born on August 26, 1878.

Despite Edgar's personal success story, and the fact that the San Luis Obispo ranches turned out to be hugely lucrative, the acquisition of these lands also set the conditions for the end of the Steele clan's expansion. Stemming from an error in one of the signatures to the Corral de Piedra ranch, a series of lawsuits over the disputed title plagued the Steeles for nearly a decade. Edgar called in his lawyer brother, George, to help him straighten out the estate's affairs in San Luis.

Throughout the 1870s, while Edgar and George were so deeply engaged in court battles, the depression that gripped the nation after the Civil War and the failure of the Bank of California drained American pocketbooks. People were desperate. California was like a pressure cooker; exacerbated by a tidal wave of immigrants still pouring into the state, the fear of not ever having enough drove men hard. Some of them resented the Steeles' achievements and coveted their property. Although the legal title to their San Luis property was eventually cleared, the Steeles were forced over time to sell much of what they owned on the Central Coast.

Norman and Fannie (Braghetta) Steele's home near the Gazos Creek. Parts of the kitchen came off the Columbia *shipwreck. Men in front are, left to right: Charles Steele Sr.; Norman Steele Sr.; Charles Bailey.*

A Dairy Empire

CASCADE RANCH AND WHITE HOUSE DAIRY

Not long after the close of the Civil War, Rensselaer's wife, Clara, 42, died at their Cascade Creek home on the last day of May in 1866. We don't know if she died from illness, accident, or if she just gave out. Their son, Eben, had died at the age of 16 from pneumonia he'd contracted after duck hunting in the cool Point Reyes marshes, and their daughter, Ella, 22, was already embarked on her adult life. She'd attended Mills College and studied music in Europe. An accomplished musician on both the organ and piano, she played at several churches in San Francisco and spent most of her time in the City. Rensselaer, nearly 58, was left with only his workmen and his relatives to keep him company.

Cascade Ranch ran from the Cascade Creek to the Gazos Creek at the north end of the Año Nuevo grant. Rensselaer was a superb dairy rancher and now that he was a widower he put all his attention into the family business. A couple of years passed and Rensselaer experienced an unexpected second springtime in his life when he remarried. His new wife, appropriately named Hattie R. Younglove, presented him with a son, Rensselaer E. Jr. on November 4, 1869.

The boy later became known as "One-Armed Steele" because of an accident he had when he was young. According to Harvey H. Mowry's book *Echoes from Gazos Creek Country* he was helping his cousin Frank Steele during mowing time when he fell into a reaper, severing his left hand and losing his right arm just below his shoulder. (A later voter registry only mentions the loss of his hand.) Rensselaer Jr. survived the incident and went on to live an active life despite his handicap.

Rensselaer Sr.'s family was expanding in other ways, too. Eight months before his new son was born, his brother Samuel "Horace" Steele, wife Amanda, and son, Charles (Charlie) Edward Steele, 18, arrived in the house on a bright March day after a long voyage by sea. Horace spotted an

Rensselaer E. Steele's thresher outfit. Early 1900s.

ideal site on the shore near Waddell's Wharf for his own house and a general store and immediately started assembling building materials.

Waddell's Wharf, a 700-foot long pier built in the cove leeward of New Year's Point, was the hub of local activity. William Waddell had built it to facilitate the shipment of lumber from his own mill not far away. In the four years since, the wharf proved to be so handy for the lumber- and dairymen all around—another option for them besides the whaling station at Pigeon Point—all the locals used it for both storage and shipping. Horace Steele put The Point New Year Store near the pier and his house on a slight knoll close by; he and Amanda moved in by February 1870.

The Point New Year Store was open seven days a week. Another of Horace's sons, Samuel Bliss Steele, came out from Ohio to join the family and worked there as an accountant and clerk. The things they sold reflect mostly the "needs," and only a few "luxuries," of the 200 souls that the store serviced. Here is a small sample, taken from records compiled by Harvey Mowry:
— Shingle nails; silk lines; hooks and guards.
— Tobacco; cigars and pipes; pocketknife.
— Broom; shirting material and linen thread; powder; candles.
— Goat slippers; undershirt, drawers and boots; cotton socks; denim pants; overalls.
— Box apples; soda crackers; sardines and meat; cane sugar and flour; peanuts.
— Ledger; books; daybook.
— 500 Upman Key and 500 Alcatras; 1 drum Eagle.
— Horse.

Horace Steele managed the store with his undivided attention for two years and then added on the task of postmaster at Año Nuevo as well. From August 1872 he worked at both jobs until his postal tenure expired in May 1874. Barely six months later he gave up storekeeping altogether, since he had moved to White House Canyon, and turned the business over to Bill Pinkham and C.P. Patterson. Pinkham and his wife, Carrie, a Pescadero woman, operated the store until it shut down in '81 or '82 while Patterson performed the very important duty of tending bar on the premises in back.

Although his dislike for politics kept Rensselaer Sr. out of the legal snarls going on down in San Luis Obispo during the '70s, his interest in his young son and in his business occupied his days. He was aging and beginning to feel it. In 1872 he asked his brother to take over the 1,000-acre White House Dairy that he'd bought in 1870. Horace Steele duly moved there in February of 1873 along with Amanda and sons Charlie and Samuel, but since he was getting on in years too, and still serving as postmaster at The Point New Year's Store, he gave the responsibility of milking 130 cows to his youngest son. Charlie, then 22, was conscientious and managed the dairy with remarkable gusto and finesse. Charlie's brother Samuel left in 1874 to work as a commission merchant for the Steele, Elder & Company in San Francisco.

On February 1, 1875 Rensselaer's daughter Ella Adeliza Steele, 31, who had been enjoying her life of music and freedom in San Francisco, officially ended her girlhood days. She had fallen in love with a Southern gentleman named Rutherford H. Brown, 36, whom she'd met in the City, and they got married. Brown was "a man of ideas" whose business interests ran from mining to land speculation. Many years later, I.C. Steele (the second) remembered him as, *"A man of medium height, slightly portly, a southern gentleman from Louisiana, very energetic, very interested in mining and ranching, and one who tended to be a bit feisty at times."*

As a wedding gift, Rensselaer Steele Sr. gave Ella and Rutherford the White House Ranch. The place had gotten its name from a two-story house painted white that was situated on a flat above the little creek. When Isaac Graham had acquired the

The whaling station at Punta de Ballena (Whale's Point), with its small Portuguese community, became transformed over the years into a critical shipping port for Coastal ranchers and loggers. The Steeles had their own warehouse located there, which they still used after Loren Coburn took possession of the wharf.

When the Carrier Pigeon *wrecked at the point, the place was renamed and in November 1872 the lighthouse was illuminated for the first time. Photos, 1900.*

Año Nuevo Rancho in the early 1850s he leased out part of it to a Mr. Van Houten, perhaps as his overseer. Van Houten ordered a pre-fabricated New England-style house to be shipped around the Horn. Once standing, the house was considered exceptionally fine for a coastal dwelling in those days—all plastered inside! However, its true claim to fame came not from its architecture but from its conspicuous location in the landscape. For decades, until a eucalyptus grove grew up around it and obscured it from view, the white house was a landmark for ships passing by to reckon the distance to San Francisco.

The Browns weren't ready to move yet, and, since Charlie Steele was handling the dairy at White House Ranch just fine, they asked him to stay on as manager. He accepted. With Charlie and his father in charge, the Browns set to constructing their own home on the property, which required moving the Graham house about 100 feet. Although several mills then in operation in nearby Gazos could have provided an abundance of first-class redwood for the project, the Browns chose to bring some of their lumber all the way around the Horn. In keeping with tradition, they painted their new house white. The Browns continued to live in San Francisco, where Rutherford conducted his mining business, and didn't come down to live at the White House Ranch until 1879.

THE SEA GILLY FLOWER

In November 1879 Rensselaer Steele Sr., at 71, was the owner of more than 2,000 acres and in poor health, but—with his daughter squared away with the White House ranch and his son due to inherit Cascade when he died—he was always ready to help out another member of the Steele family. In March, Charlie Steele, who'd managed the White House dairy for the past six years, married Alexander and Adaline Moore's only daughter, Ida Jane Moore. Naturally, Charlie and Ida wanted a place of their own but they didn't have enough cash to invest. Rensselaer bought back the 2,116-acre Wallace Ramsay Ranch that had been purchased from the Steele brothers and Horace Gushee in the mid-1860s by Ramsay and H.B. Sprague. The property included "a narrow, spring-fed ravine" that ran along the coast about a half-mile south of where the Gazos Creek (named for the Clove Pink or Sea Gilly flower that grew in that area) flows into the ocean. Rensselaer leased the land out to various people, including a 755-acre parcel of dairy ranch to Charlie with an option to buy.

Rensselaer placed a lot of trust in "tall, lean, affable, and ambitious" Charlie for he knew his nephew was a man of "much determination and foresight." For her part, Ida, "a comely lass of 23," was "equally resolute and aspiring." The young couple moved in late November to the property that "… included five buildings, a two-story house, a large dairy-house, a big barn and two smaller storage sheds." (Harvey Mowry).

Things moved very quickly after this. Charlie's parents, Amanda and Samuel H. Steele, moved in with them in December; in late January, 1880, Ida gave birth to their first child, a daughter they named Mae, and on October 8, 1881 their son Norman was born. Meanwhile Charlie worked long strenuous hours milking about 100 head daily. Help was expensive and not always available,

Rutherford H. Brown (1839 – 1897), founder of Willowside Farm, married Ella Adeliza Steele (1844 – 1919). Ella inherited White House Ranch from her father, Rensselaer Steele. Photos ca. 1875.

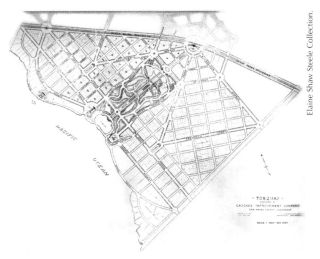

Townside map of Torquay, proposed by the Cascade Improvement Company, taken from a brochure of Torquay and California Redwood park (before 1906).

but Charlie managed to clear a profit by hiring itinerant Chinese workers to do the routine work of grubbing brush, building fences, and freshening up the paint at $.50-1.00 a day. On November 25, 1880 Charlie and Ida bought their ranch using loans from Uncle Rensselaer Steele and Rutherford Brown, and $1,000 of their own savings. From that day the place was known as the Gazos Ranch.

With Charlie gone from the White House dairy, Ella and Rutherford Brown returned from San Francisco. The Browns never had children and Rutherford must have had to put the energy that would have gone into parenting somewhere else. The man would not rest until he had acquired Willowside Ranch, a 1,100-acre dairy about three miles north of Pescadero once owned by Thomas Moore. For the rest of his life, Rutherford made himself busy on both ranches and in town—serving as Vice County Supervisor for the Pescadero area for a while—as well as overseeing his other investments. Perhaps a victim of his own best quality of character, his infinite capacity to over-commit himself to whatever he started, he died of apoplexy at age 58 on August 19, 1897 while working at Willowside. Ella had her home at White House

Ranch, her memories, her music, and family to sustain her, and she lived on without the company of her Southern gentleman for nearly 22 years more.

A Town Called Torquay

"I don't know if it's pronounced Tor-KAY or Tor-KEE. It was on the Rensselaer Steele place, the Cascade Ranch. There's a place west of the road [Cabrillo Highway] where Rensselaer Steele was going to establish this little town, but then when the earthquake hit in 1906 and the Ocean Shore Railroad went defunct, it just never materialized. My father remembered a post office that was already built there, but I don't remember it."
— Ruth Moore

Rensselaer Steele Sr. died Nov. 6, 1886 at age 78. Rensselaer Jr.—"One-Armed Steele"—took over Cascade and also had a farm machinery business in San Francisco. In the next 14 years the Ocean Shore Railroad occupied his thoughts. Like other businessmen living along the coast—Loren Coburn among them—Rensselaer knew that if the rail came through all the way from San Francisco to Santa Cruz, the opportunities for growth and development in the area were limitless. He invested heavily in the railroad and then in the early 1900s mortgaged his ranch for $60,000 so he could sub-divide the land and build a resort town on it.

Rensselaer was unlucky. Torquay town was surveyed and some lots had already been sold when the 1906 earthquake eventually put the railroad and Rensselaer immediately out of business. He turned over his mortgage to Humphrey with the stipulation that he could live out his life at Cascade on an allowance of "so much per month."

Humphrey also bought White House Ranch from Rensselaer's widowed half-sister, Ella Brown. As a testament to the good relationship established over the years between Humphrey and the Steeles, she, too, was allowed to live out her days in her home until she passed away in 1919. Rensselaer, who married and divorced one woman without having issue, lived to see 65, surviving the years of the First World War, the Spanish flu, the Roaring Twenties, and enough of the Depression to subdue anyone's spirits. He died at Cascade on September 11, 1935.

GREEN OAKS CREEK RANCH

Isaac Chapman Steele was in his early 40s when he moved from Point Reyes to New Year's Point. He and his wife, cousin Hulda, settled very comfortably in their handsome Greek Revival house at Green Oaks. His Ohio-born children, Frederick and Effie, were respectively 17 and 13 years old. George Horace, born in Petaluma, was three.

Isaac's life was very full. Like his brothers down in San Luis Obispo, he was deeply engaged with the agrarian cause and a leader in the Grange movement. The Grange had its roots in a rising discontent that had begun in the mid-1800s among farm communities. Hounded by bankers and hostile railroad companies, farmers organized the Patrons of Husbandry under the direction of a man named O.H. Kelly, probably about the same time the Grange Legislation passed in 1870. Borrowing ritual from the Masonic Lodge, the Patrons became a permanent organization in 1873. The California State Grange also came into being that same year, Pescadero #32 representing San Mateo County.

Along with the Weeks, the Moores, and other local families, Isaac Steele believed that "Debt is the farmer's curse." With them he worked diligently to create a legal structure for farmers to achieve solvency and became Master of the state organization in 1879. From this position he strongly advocated agricultural education at the college and university levels and was a primary agent in founding a post office that served the farmers' needs. By 1900 the Grange had been instrumental in passing an impressive range of legislation to improve the farmer's lot that included anti-trust laws; the establishment of Postal Savings Banks; pure food laws; and election of US senators by popular vote.

One of Isaac's sympathizers and moral supporters at Green Oaks was S.J. Finney. Finney was married to Mary B. Steele, Isaac's cousin and widow of his half-brother Osman Steele, who had been killed while serving as Deputy Sheriff during the Anti-Rent Riot in New York. Mary and Osman had had one son, also named Osman N. Steele, who at this point was an adult and helping to run a section of the Green Oaks Ranch.

Finney was interested in doing good works, especially in

Chloe Worden Steele, (1848 – 1934) Frederick Nathaniel Steele's wife. Photographed in San Francisco by Theo C. Marceau. Ca. 1860

Isaac Chapman Steele (1820 – 1903) from a copy supplied by Catherine Baumgarten Steele.

Fred Steele with Clara, Emma, Will and maybe Flora Steele in front of their house. Ca. 1886.

I.C. Steele could play a "fair tune." Ca. 1888.

education. While serving as the State Senator from San Mateo County, and abetted by the Steele boys down in San Luis Obispo, Finney introduced the Compulsory Education Bill in the Senate. Sadly, according to Catherine Baumgarten Steele, he was a good politician but not a good dairyman. He was smart enough to take a hint and shifted from dairy farming to raising grain early in 1875. Later that year his son Will died at 20 of cerebral meningitis. Despondent over family troubles and grieving deeply over his son's death, Finney committed suicide on July 27, 1875 and was buried at the Mount Hope cemetery in Pescadero. Osman Steele Jr. continued to run the ranch until 1914, when he sold it. The property eventually passed into the possession of David Atkins, who renamed it Coastways Ranch. Descendants of Atkins' family still own Coastways today.

At Green Oaks things ran fairly smoothly under the direction of Isaac and his oldest son, Frederick Nathaniel Steele. Frederick farmed the 500 acres of the home place but, because his health was poor, his main responsibilities were restricted to keeping the books and supervising. In 1869, at age 23, he married Chloe Worden. They had four children: Isaac Chapman Steele (named after his grandfather, he was known as "I.C."); Clara; Emma; and William.

Frederick was musically inclined like many of the Steeles and played the violin. He encouraged his children to appreciate music, too, and since they had no radio, nor a concert hall nearby, they put together an impromptu family orchestra for their own entertainment. Frederick and I.C. played violin; a sister played piano and pump organ; and an uncle played cello. Sometimes they traveled to Pescadero to play for the Grange dances.

In later years I.C. Steele remembered that one of his relatives' close associates of old up at the Ramsay Ranch, H.B. Sprague, was a good musician. He, too, played the violin, reputed to be a very fine Stradivarius. When Sprague died he was living in San Francisco; Frederick Steele went to the City and bought the instrument to bring home for his son. I.C. modestly claimed he could play "a fair tune on it."

Frederick, 61, died on September 24, 1907; Chloe outlived him by another 27 years. She also outlived her two unmarried daughters, Clara and Emma, both of whom died within three days of each other in 1920, victims of the great Spanish flu pandemic.

Edward Conant, a resident in the area at that time, remembers the epidemic vividly. *"I was living at Pigeon Point when World War I ended and the terrible flu was raging. We wore homemade masks from many thicknesses of cheesecloth to prevent us from catching [it]. I don't think it did much good. We were told to burn sulphur on top of the old wood stove and breathe the smoke fumes and that would kill the flu germs. We tried anything and everything, as there was no medicine in those days that you could get or take for the flu epidemic. Many died...I lost two cousins from it. Our family of six all had it but one. We all made it through."*

Chloe's sons, I.C., 35, and William, 24, stayed on after their father's death and took over separate farms of the old Green Oaks Ranch.

Life was not always posing for formal pictures. Life was for having fun, too. Here, three young women and their escorts are surf fishing at Perch Rock in the 1890s.

A 100-Year Legacy

LIFE AT GREEN OAKS

Isaac Chapman Steele ("I.C."), Frederick and Chloe Worden Steele's first child, was born on November 5, 1872 in the family's home at Green Oaks. At this point the Steeles had been doing dairy in the Pescadero coastal area for almost 10 years. The ranch was isolated, but, with I.C.'s folks and all the Steele relatives and people who lived on neighboring ranches, Año Nuevo had the semblance of a cohesive coastal "community" that was defined by its own self-generated activities of dairy ranching and farming, whaling and fishing, shipping, logging and milling.

I.C.'s birth year was remarkable. The newly constructed lighthouse at Pigeon Point turned on its Fresnel light for the first time a couple of weeks after he was born. Loren Coburn assumed ownership of the Pigeon Point land the Steeles had formerly leased and he actually moved there from San Francisco to take charge of the shipping operations

I.C. with a buck and Monte, a horse belonging to Alec Moore. I.C. Steele lived a little over a 100 years. In his lifetime he saw many changes to the Coastal way of life.

at its wharf, destined in the coming years to play an increasingly aggressive role in the economics of the whole Pescadero region. In this year, too, Alexander Gordon initiated construction of a 100-foot-long chute on the bluffs at Tunitas Creek with the intention of creating another port on the Coast. It burned down in 1885.

Inset:
James Harvey, a familiar stagedriver on the Coastal route. Ca. 1902.

Right:
A peddler's wagon on the Coastal route.

Pescadero, somewhat less remote than Santa Cruz, offered services and a social life to anyone who had reason and time to get there. For the Coast residents such occasions were limited, but for many years a stagecoach pulled by two sweating, straining horses that came through every day over the dirt track helped to keep them connected.

The stagecoach line, also founded in 1872 by a Santa Cruz man named "Billy" Bias, went from Santa Cruz to Pescadero, where another stage line linked it to the San Gregorio/Redwood City segment, carrying passengers and "delivering everything from needles and spools of thread for coast housewives, to sacks of flour and shovels for their husbands."

In I.C.'s estimation, traveling to Santa Cruz was always a "four-hour ordeal of mud holes in winter and dust clouds in summer." Stage drivers got worn out quick. Billy Bias lasted only a couple of years then sold the line to a Pescadero man, Nathan Ingalls. Ingalls did better, holding on until 1890 when he sold the business to 32-year-old Charles L. Littlefield.

Littlefield, born in Maine, had been in California since 1870 and did some lumbering before moving to Santa Cruz in 1890. He seemed to have found his niche with the stagecoach line and ran it for 12 years, driving the north half of the Santa Cruz/Pescadero route himself. This leg started at Swanton, did a slow pull up Gianone Hill, then switch-backed down to Waddell Creek.

From here the going got rough. The "high, bald-faced cliffs of Waddell Canyon's north wall terminated abruptly at sea edge and effectively barred north and south traffic except at low tide." The only way to get around these cliffs was a tricky 3/4-mile stretch of sand beach with a particularly hazardous rocky spit known as "Cape Horn" midway between the entry and exit points. Most often the teamsters would have to pick-and-shovel their way through piles of rock rubble that had fallen from the cliffs above. From there, Littlefield continued on past the Green Oaks, White House, and Gazos ranches to Pigeon Point, maybe picking up a small batch of cheese at the Steeles before finishing his run at Pescadero.

Littlefield got comfortable with his adventurous job on the Coast and liked to indulge in gentle fun with his passengers' nerves. I.C. Steele said that Littlefield used to let everybody get out to stretch their legs after an especially rough ride. Before getting back up in the driver's seat he'd pull out a whiskey bottle full of brown liquid and swig it down, never letting on that it was only tea!

Littlefield became well acquainted with the people who lived on his route and in 1892 he married Mary Reed, the daughter of James Reed, who owned a ranch outside Pescadero. He continued to drive stage for another 10 years and then sold it to James Harvey in 1902. As proof of his sanguine nature, Littlefield then moved with his family to the Pigeon Point area to work for Loren Coburn and became one of the local Pescadero regulars.

I.C.'s birth marked the beginning of a challenging decade. As has been mentioned elsewhere, California was in the early stages of a financial depression and the situation would worsen in 1875 when the Bank of California failed. Wages were low and most people were poor. On top of droughts, crop failures, riots in the cities, squatter wars, racial hate crimes (particularly against the Chinese), price fixing, and company stock failures that pressed upon the common people, the mighty Central Pacific Railroad and its subsidiaries had a stranglehold on state and local governments.

Through hard work and loyalty to the clan, the Steeles managed to keep their heads above water. The sheer size of their property holdings and the solid infrastructure they'd established to sustain their enterprises also gave the Steeles a reasonable buffer against insolvency.

Everybody worked, in whatever capacity each could. When he was old enough, I.C. rode his horse out to the pastures, rounding up as many as

104 cows at a time, and driving them back to the barn. Horace Steele's Point New Year Store was up and running at the Waddell Wharf; the Steele ranches continued to produce grain, cheese, and butter in huge quantities and shipped their products out of Point New Year, Pigeon Point, and Gazos Creek to a city market that facilitated wider distribution.

Still, cash was scarce; it was the land—and its creatures—that fed them. Hunting was a routine affair. Deer, quail, and ducks were still plentiful and fishing holes were handy. People pulled salmon, sardines, crab, and tuna out of the creeks and the ocean. A few grizzlies still roamed the wooded canyons, occasionally scaring people to shelter behind the closed doors of their cabins, but they were fast disappearing. The last incident recorded of a fatal bear encounter in the area was in 1875, when William Waddell—the well-known lumberman and architect of the wharf at New Year's Point—lost his life from wounds inflicted in a hand-to-paw battle with one of them.

Whale oil was still being used for fuel during I.C.'s time and the Portuguese at the little village at Pigeon Point engaged in shore whaling well into the '90s. One day when I.C. was about 24 he was driving a horse and cart to Pescadero when he saw them in the waters offshore.

"They were out in a 30-foot boat and they had just harpooned a whale—one of the biggest I ever saw. I sat and watched while that whale dragged that boat. He was going so fast the boat came clear out of the water and went flying through the air! Those whalers had offered to take me out with them sometime, but when I saw that I changed my mind. They finally had to cut the line and let that whale go." (Koch interview)

Remnants of the "fur trade" still existed when I.C. was a boy. Seals were a favorite of one neighbor who made his living by *"slaughtering seals and selling the hides and whiskers to the Chinese people in San Francisco. The hides were used for making shoes and the stiff whiskers were used as handles for ear-clean-*

Opposite: *Pescadero, 1900. The I.D.E.S. chapel is present at this time but you can't see it. The hall has not yet been built.*

Right: *Ladies walk past the former Methodist Episcopalian Church in Pescadero town. 1900.*

ing spoons and such. The longer the whiskers, the more valuable they were."

Before I.C. was 10, there was a brief time when sea otters, too, still lived along that stretch of the coast. But with no limits on the take, the otters were completely cleaned out within a couple of years. I.C. said that the "hunters" would anchor their schooners in Año Nuevo Bay and go out in small boats for a shooting spree, their guns popping like firecrackers on the Fourth of July.

Other "sports" that could be enjoyed required more skill. Louis McCormick, in a 1923 historical piece he wrote for the Pescadero school paper, *The Carnelian*, tells that, *"Another sport quite different from hunting was breaking wild horses. All of the young men of the day considered it great fun to lasso a wild bronco and after a short but stormy trip get spilled all over the landscape. Most of this took place on the Coburn grant [Steele ranches], which was then a cattle ranch and a part of the wild and woolly west of fifty years ago."*

The local people were resourceful in other ways, too. In 1896 the steamer *Columbia* went aground just south of Pigeon Point. The vessel was loaded with Christmas cargo—"dress goods, cases of olive oil, all sorts of things." As the ship went to pieces, the cargo floated ashore and the thrifty locals salvaged anything they could. They used scraps of wood and metal to build sheds or fencing, or an extra room in back of the house. The biggest bonanza was a large load of white lead from the ship's hold. Soon, almost every home on the coast shone clean and bright with a new coat of paint.

"CHINESE LAUNDRY"

As most people schooled in California history know, Chinese men immigrated by the thousands to work the gold fields in the early 1850s, and later to build the Central Pacific Railroad. They were not afraid of hard work or privation, and were marvelously open to opportunities that other people might not even see. As a result, from their

At left, *a newspaper cartoon strip found in Grace Shaw's memory album illustrates the general mood in California against people of Chinese ancestry in the late 1800s. In spite of this, racism did not always rule the practice when farmers hired workers. On the Steele ranches Chinese were hired early on and often became integral members of the Coastal community.*

Lower left, *Ah Sing, the hired man at Green Oaks, practices his hunting skills, caught in a moment with his rifle still smoking. At lower right another worker at the Green Oaks dairy watches over the water-powered separator in the creamery. At right,* is an informal shot of a man who might be Ah Sing.

first arrival in this country, the Chinese suffered from bitter resentment, persecution, and discrimination at the hands of Americans.

The great majority of these immigrants were single men seeking higher wages than they could earn in their homeland, or any wages at all; when they'd saved enough, they intended to return to their wives and children. Easily recognizable as being "foreign" by their physical characteristics, dress, and customs, the Chinese could not integrate readily into American society and usually banded together. They developed services and social groups within their own mini-communities in an effort to sustain as normal a life as possible. They bunked together, spoke their own language, bought cooked food from their own vendors, goods at their own stores, and got their clothes washed at their own laundry.

Nevertheless, their lives in California were not always unhappy. The Chinese began to appear on the Coast in the 1860s, but, according to historian Sandy Lydon, they concentrated first in the Santa Cruz area in the early 1850s as abalone fishermen. In those days most Caucasians didn't even think abalone was good to eat, but it was a food highly prized by the Chinese. A delicacy enjoyed and fished for hundreds of years, China's resources were tapped out. The Chinese, delighted to discover that abalone was abundant in the Monterey Bay and Coastal waters north of Santa Cruz, were the first to develop it commercially.

The Chinese people also harvested sea bird eggs. In the early 1850s eggs of any kind were very hard to find and consequently very expensive in San Francisco markets. The Chinese started from the Farallones and worked their way down the Coast, harvesting even such oddities as cormorant eggs from the off-shore rocks.

In the mid- to late 1860s the Chinese turned to logging and agriculture, working as seasonal laborers in the crop fields on the Coast. Many dairy and farm ranches in California had grown by this time to the size of "baronial estates." The work that needed to be done demanded a labor force that far exceeded the capacity of individual ranch owners and their families. There simply weren't enough people. As the resident labor force of Mexican and Native workers was gone, operations as big as the Steeles' looked to the hard-working Chinese men.

The Steeles, like other local ranchers and milling operators in the area, accomplished this through go-between agents who contracted out of a San Francisco company. Sometimes these workers stayed on for years in the Steeles' employment as trusted members of their "extended family."

Two of the workers who were employed full time by Charlie Steele between 1883 and 1892 are a case in point. "Charley Cook" assisted Ida with the cooking and other chores around the house; Ah Hoy worked in the dairy as a milker, making butter and cheese. Ah Hoy also kept an eye on the young Steele lads, Norman and Grover, when they were underfoot. The boys used to imitate Ah Hoy's pidgin English and learned to converse with him in this language. The man grew very fond of them. In 1894 Ah Hoy went back to China to visit his family and wrote letters to the Steeles expressing his fervent wish to return to the Gazos Ranch as soon as he could make enough money to do so, but the letters finally lapsed and Ah Hoy never came back.

Ah Hoy's lack of funds must not have been the only factor preventing his return. Since the 1870s hatred towards the Chinese had grown into a movement of such intensity that it culminated in legislation passed in 1882 that barred entry to the United States by any Chinese citizen—the first and only time in American history that foreign immigration was specifically restricted by "race." With the Chinese Exclusion Act in place, Ah Hoy had no hope of ever becoming a naturalized citizen.

THE GAZOS CREEK SCHOOL

As a boy I.C. studied with his brother, Will, and the cheesemaker's daughter in the small schoolhouse at Green Oaks privately run by the Steeles. It had its own desks and books, a wood stove for heat, and a hired teacher who lived with the family. When he was 20, I.C. took courses at Chestnutwood's Business College in Santa Cruz and boarded in town. Perhaps it was at this time that his life interests started to shift away from dairy ranching to farming and growing fruit. Later in 1905, when his Uncle Rensselaer was setting up the new town at Torquay, I.C. planned to supply its markets with his own homegrown apples. Even though the Torquay scheme failed, by 1910 I.C.'s orchards were well established.

In the early 1890s the Coastlanders built another schoolhouse at the mouth of Gazos Creek, about half a mile north of Charlie Steele's ranch. Besides the Steeles—Will, Clara and Emma Steele, and Flora Dickerman—there were two Milrick boys, and a couple of Manley kids. Their teacher was a gentle, sweet-mannered 18-year-old from Half Moon Bay named Sarah Louise Compton. Louise had taught at Bellvale, a little one-room school up La Honda way, before she came to Gazos. She boarded at the Steele's Green Oaks house and it was there she met her future husband, I.C. Steele. They waited until after I.C. finished college to get married.

Nine young women taught at the Gazos School in the '90s and into the early 1900s. Most of the teachers boarded at one of the local ranches because their own homes were too far away. Miss Huff came from Pescadero; Louise Compton and Ida Jackson came from Half Moon Bay and both stayed at Green Oaks. When school was in session, one of the Steeles would carry the teacher in an old horse-drawn cart over the dirt road to Gazos.

Sometimes there were as many as 20 students enrolled in the school. The children came

Mrs. Ellis taught I.C., Clara and Emma. Late 1870s or early 1880s.

Louise Compton. Ca. 1891.

Miss Brown; Clara and Emma Steele; Miss Jackson. Miss Jackson taught at the Gazos (Pigeon Point) school and boarded with the I.C. Steeles. Miss Brown may also have been one of the schoolteachers. Early to mid-1890s.

from the families living at Pigeon Point, Bean Hollow, and from the ranches and sawmills tucked back in the woods.

Edward Conant, who attended Gazos Creek School between 1916 and 1918, remembers that sometimes his mother brought him the four miles to school in a horse and buggy. *"The ruts in the road were so deep one stayed in the ruts. The mud was so bad in these ruts that the wagon wheels would pick up big chunks and it would drop off the wheels."* But he would often have to walk. Sometimes he would get lucky when a hauling truck would come by and pick him up. In the winter he appreciated this very much because, *"It was so cold the horses' watering troughs were frozen over and icicles were hanging from the branches of trees."*

The schoolhouse burned down in about 1920 and a new one was built a little farther up the Gazos Canyon. Another young teacher, Miss Catherine Baumgarten, from Texas, came to teach at the second school in 1922. Just as it had worked for Louise Compton, serendipity again brought together two young people because of their association with the school. Catherine later married I.C.'s younger brother, William Steele.

STANLEY STEELE OF CHALK RIDGE ORCHARD

In 1905, two years after Louise gave birth to their first child, Muriel, I.C. started building the house at Chalk Ridge Orchard near his father's Green Oaks home. Louise figured out the lumber and ordered it from Waddell's mill. When the earthquake of 1906 struck California the house wasn't finished yet. Years later, in an interview with Margaret Koch done days before his 100th birthday, I.C. recalled that, *"The frame was up and the partitions were in. When the 'quake came along it shook everything, of course, and it shook the house out of square—really racked it."* He went on to tell that his carpenter friend, Bernard Scofield, came by to visit not long afterwards. *"Bernard stood silently for a long time, just looking at the crooked house but not saying a word.*

I finally said to him, 'Yes, Bernard, I know it's out of square. The earthquake did it.' And Bernard said, 'Well, just so you know. I wasn't going to say anything.'"

I.C. persevered, and he and Louise moved into their beautiful new home. Sometime during this period, between 1903 and 1906, Louise had been pregnant with a second child. The experience she'd had delivering Muriel in her own bed had gone so smoothly, she wanted to have the next one at home, too. But the breech baby was born dead, its umbilical cord wrapped around its neck, and the birthing was so hard Louise nearly died along with the child. When she became pregnant again, she resolved to give birth with a doctor in attendance so she went to Pescadero where her son, Stanley, was born on November 18, 1907 in William Knapp's house.

As a youngster Stanley rode a pony up the dirt road that led to the same school at Gazos Canyon where his mother had taught. He did well in his elementary school studies and went to Santa Cruz for his first year in high school. In 1922 he switched up to Pescadero town and entered the second class (Class of '24) to graduate from the new Pescadero Union High School. Stanley joined the boys' basketball team and played with teammates and friends Henry, Loren, Claude and Graham McCormick; Eddie Blomquist; Clarence Frey; Lester Pinkham; and John Nixon. Sometimes he wrote articles for the school newspaper, *The Carnelian*, and the *Pescadero Pebble*. His stories covered what the boys did at Christmastime (trap skunks and wild cats), fishing expeditions, and field trips sponsored by the school.

Among his younger schoolmates was Carol Shaw; she was an active, outdoor kind of person, too, and their common interests and the long association between their families allowed shy, quiet Stanley an opportunity to become better friends. He started asking her to go with him to the school dances and paying visits to her at her home on the Shaw Ranch. Little did he know at the time that it

Top, *box label and apple wrapper logo for fruit grown at Chalk Ridge Orchard (I.C. Steele Ranch)*; above, *I.C. and Lou Steele's Chalk Ridge Orchard house*; below, *Stanley Steele and Earle Williamson. Ca. 1912.*

would be Carol's younger sister, Elaine—the young Shaw girl giggling behind her hand when he came in the door—that he would marry a few years down the road.

Fate presented different paths to both Stanley and Carol. Stanley wanted to become an architect but after he graduated from high school he was obliged to go back to the Chalk Ridge ranch to help his father. People on the Coast were abandoning dairying and turning to agriculture. They needed more water for crops such as artichokes, and Stanley found work helping to construct a flume on the Gazos Creek. Meanwhile, Carol graduated a little later than Stanley and went to stay with her Aunt Bertha and Uncle Ben Blaisdell in Santa Cruz. She went out for a while with one of Stanley's cousins, Charlie and Ida Steele's son, Norman, before she met and married her husband, Lee Stevens, in Santa Cruz.

Stanley and his father grew peas, beans, oats and hay for their horses. Elaine Shaw remarks that, "[I.C.] never set the world on fire—he never really had to do anything." He was a "gentleman farmer" and didn't like to get his hands dirty; Stanley, however, was a hands-on kind of man and worked at everything—machinery, animal husbandry, hunting, and fishing. He wouldn't give up on his dream of becoming an architect, though, and made time to take post-graduate classes in technical drawing at Pescadero High School to prepare for that career. Then the Depression stopped him.

A REALLY GOOD LIFE

Elaine Shaw graduated from high school in 1933. As we learned from her story, Elaine and Stanley got married in 1936. Stanley's intentions were for them to move up to Elaine's old home outside Pescadero and raise their family on the Shaw Ranch. That seemed to be the most practical way to weather the tough financial times and create a peaceful life on his own terms.

Their first child, Ruth Louise Steele, was

born in 1938 in a Santa Cruz hospital. For a short time when she was very small, she and her parents did live up on the Shaw Ranch outside Pescadero where her mother had grown up. The amenities weren't fancy: they used an outhouse instead of indoor facilities and Elaine cooked on a wood stove. Ruth remembers that her mother was a good cook in the English style—very plain, everything boiled, without using too many herbs or spices—but on her birthday, Ruth would sometimes get angel food cake as a treat.

But Stanley was never really able to get away from Chalk Ridge. I.C. was "really mad" when Stanley and Elaine moved to the Shaw Ranch with plans to make it their permanent home. He needed his son's help in his own fields and orchards. The couple had only been gone a few months when Stanley's mother, "Lulu" or "Lou," became bedridden after she had a stroke and lost a leg. Stanley and family moved back to the house east of Green Oaks Ranch at Chalk Ridge Orchard to take care of her and to help his father on the farm.

This may have been a blessing in disguise for Elaine, who had grown up without the loving guidance of her own mother. Elaine says her mother-in-law was a lovely person. *"She was such a delightful, beautiful, oh, really a beautiful person. Never found fault. Nana was very quiet and sweet-natured, like [Stanley]."* Elaine cared for Lou intensively for two years until she was well enough to move around a bit on her own or with the help of a wheelchair, and then for another five years beyond that. When Elaine had her first baby, Ruth, she would go to Lou for advice but the older woman would always tell Elaine she was doing just fine, whatever she decided would be right.

Added to the condition of Lou's health, I.C. probably wanted to keep Stanley and Elaine close to him for another reason. Stanley's sister, Muriel, had died in 1934 and her husband, Harry Olund, in 1938. Their son, Andy Olund, came to live as a permanent member of I.C.'s household at Chalk Ridge

Top: *Stanley Steele.*
Middle: *Stanley with Grandma Chloe, sister Muriel, mom Lou, and his nephew, Andy Olund.*
Bottom: *Stanley's young wife, Elaine Shaw Steele, at home on a tractor.*

Inset: *Elaine Steele takes a break.*
Above right: *I.C. Steele and wife Lou, with their grandchildren: from left, Ruth Louise Steele; Sandra Jean Steele; and Andy Olund. August 1941.*

after his father died, and was being raised by his grandparents. Ruth, her sister Sandra—born in 1940—and their cousin, Andy, would grow up together with their parents and grandparents in their grandparents' house.

"*Andy's nine years older than I am,*' Ruth says, "*and when he came to us I was just a baby, too little to remember him much when I was growing up. His mother—my aunt—died on the operating table when he was five. I guess his father never really got over that, and then he himself was killed in an automobile accident just four years later, so Andy was orphaned when he was nine. It was really my grandmother and grandfather who raised him, rather than my parents.*

"*Andy wasn't into farming. He is good at gardening, though. Andy has a beautiful garden, and that part I think he got from Granddad. I do remember walking down the road with Andy to catch the school bus when I was going to Pigeon Point School in first and second grades. He must have been in high school by then. I remember he had BIG feet—he is a tall man now! I think it [his parents' early deaths] affected him a lot, and he kind of kept to himself.*"

Stanley held on to the Shaw Ranch and farmed it for years, splitting his time between working there and at Chalk Ridge. Not having the extra money for hired help, Stanley had to do all the work himself. Driving back and forth every day, he left the house early in the morning and came back home again late at night. Ruth didn't see much of her father.

"[My Dad] never was in the Army. I don't know what the deal was, but during the war, the farmers might have been exempt. My mother told me that they didn't have much money; Dad used to chop wood and sell cords of wood so we could have shoes on our feet. But then the flax years were good and things were better. That was in the '40s, and after the War."

Stanley was a dry farmer and had been since he was a teenager. Since the early '20s the Coast had gone through a period of drought years that forced many of the dairymen to convert to dry farming. The farmers put in oats, hay, grain and vetch. Ruth remembers that during her childhood and teen-age years her father grew a lot of flax, a favored crop at the time that filled a demand for

Clockwise from top, the Shaw girls re-united: Elaine Shaw Steele with daughter Ruth Louise, 1; cousin Maria Adair Stewart and son Peter, 17 months; Ruth Shaw Elliott and JoAnn Stewart, 3; Carol Shaw Stevens and daughter Carol Lee, 10 months. April 16, 1939.

linen and linseed oil. Stanley's hard work paid off finally when Ruth was about five or six years old. The lovely blue-flowered fields of flax brought in enough profit for Stanley and Elaine to buy the Shaw Ranch from Uncle John, Aunt Carol, and Aunt Ruth sometime near the end of the War. It remained in their hands until they sold it sometime after 1960.

When Ruth was very small she spent a lot of time with her grandfather, and, whenever she could, her father, both of whom she adored.

"That's the reason I'm interested in flowers and birds; it was my grandfather's influence," she remarked recently. "He was a very good gardener. He would start redwood trees from slips and did a lot of grafting of trees. My father did, too.

"In around 1910, I think it was, my grandfather was shipping apples. There was a huge orchard—that was the business my grandfather was in—it's completely gone, now. And they raised chickens and sold chicken eggs. One of my jobs was cleaning out the chicken coops, which I didn't appreciate.

"Table manners were very important to my Granddad. If you put your elbows on the table—I sat next to him—boy, he would rap with a knife on your elbow if I put my elbows on the table. And you had to clean your plate. And you had to wait until he got to the table before we could start eating.

"I remember one time, he had this beautiful garden going, and I got mad at him. I don't know how old I was. I pulled up all of his carrots, and beets. I just pulled them all up. I was in big trouble. [laughs] And I never forgot it. He didn't really do too much, but I got in a lot of trouble with my folks.

"But [I loved] just being with him. He always had

Ruth in her garden.

The Steele Family

Insets: *Stanley Steele sews grain sacks of barley or oats, supervised by "Mike" the hound; in August 1950, Ruth Louise and Sandra play on sacks at the Shaw Ranch with cousins Carol Lee, Lynne, Susan and Elaine.*

Below: *Uncle Lee's Studebaker truck; "Mike;" Stanley; Ruth; and Carol Lee Stevens; Bob Elliott (Ruth Shaw's husband) and Lynne Elliott; Sandra Jean Steele at Shaw Ranch.*

different *types of trees growing down there—guava trees, avocado trees, loquat trees. He taught me to eat the pineapple guava flowers, just the petals. They were real sweet and good.*

"I loved to be with my father. I was driving tractor when I was 9. He just gave me the keys and told me to take it out in the field. That's how I learned. I think I was about 9 or 10 [when I started on] the wheel tractor, but the power wagon, I was probably about 12 or 13. I helped my Dad sew [grain] sacks when I was about 12."

All photos by Lee Stevens from: Elaine Shaw Steele Collection.

162 *Portraits of Pescadero*

Ruth went to the same one-room school at Gazos Creek—right in back of Pinky's (the Beach House)—that her father had attended when he was a boy and where her grandmother had been a teacher. Ruth was the only girl in first and second grades. Then, because there were only 12 students in her class, she was skipped over two grades and sent to Pescadero to start fourth grade. A school bus that drove down as far as the San Mateo county line at Año Nuevo picked her up every day and brought her home in the afternoon.

At first going in to Pescadero every weekday was a strange experience for Ruth—"*I was scared to death, because I'd never seen so many kids in all my life!*"—but she made good friends right away. In grade school she rarely got the chance to play with them after classes though, because she had to catch the bus to go home.

Ruth's best childhood companion was her sister Sandra. Their home life was very much like what their mother, Elaine, experienced when she was growing up on the Shaw Ranch: there weren't any other kids in the neighborhood, nobody to just drop in for an hour or two, but there was family. Although each had her own special interests, Ruth and Sandra became very close friends.

"*We called Sandra 'The Housefly.' She was always playing with her dolls. Dorothy Williamson was her teacher and Dorothy always had beautiful long nails; Sandra used to put Scotch tape on her fingernails and pretend to be Dorothy Williamson teaching her dolls at school. But I was always outside with my dog, Ginger.*

"*We were very active in 4-H. When I was growing up I raised pigs. I named one 'Puggy-Wo.' We did not win prizes, just raised them and then sold them. My sister raised a steer. And she was into horses. I wasn't interested in horses; horses are too big. I was more interested in driving the power wagon and things like that. Being on the tractor.*

"*I took sewing with 4-H from Mrs. Binger. I hate sewing, my jaw always locks up. I'd rather be outside. At one time I thought I would learn how to crochet so when I'm older I'd have something I could do when I couldn't work outside. But my jaw was so clenched, and the chain stitch was so tight, that I gave it up. I said, 'This isn't for me.'*"

Big social occasions fell on holidays, events that were usually attended by Elaine's Shaw family members, their spouses and children. Elaine had always kept close touch with her sisters, Carol Shaw Stevens and Ruth Shaw Elliott, and with her cousin, Maria Adair Stewart. The Shaw women

Top: *The second generation of "Shaw" girls are, left to right, Ruth Steele; Carol Lee Stevens; Sandra Steele; Lynne Elliott; Susan Stevens; and Elaine Elliott.*

Above, left: *Sandra and Carol Lee accompany Ruth playing the guitar Granddad I.C. gave her when she was six years old. 1952.*

Above, right: *Sandra, 12, with "Freddie Cow-Cow." 1952.*

each had two girls, and these six girls especially formed the next generation of cousins who would grow up to be lifelong friends.

Fourth of July picnics at Green Oaks were grand. Family members would team up and play baseball—Elaine could "clobber" that ball!— and kids and adults would help Stanley finish bringing in the new-mown hay. Later there would be fireworks down at the beach.

The biggest get-together of the year was Thanksgiving at the Shaw Ranch with Carol's family, the Stevenses. Stanley and Uncle Lee would go quail-hunting in the morning; Aunt Carol always made sugared grapes. The girl cousins would stuff themselves yet miraculously survive every time. *"We used to think that was wonderful, even though she would use egg whites and you're not supposed to do that [because of] salmonella. It's a wonder we didn't die."*

Except for the three kids going to school, and Stanley driving up to the Shaw Ranch to work, the Steeles didn't go in to Pescadero town much.

"We had our own eggs; we had our own vegetables," Ruth says. *"We bought flour, sugar, and all that kind of stuff, stocked on hand, so you just didn't [go]. And there was gas rationing then, too, when I was growing up."*

They didn't go to church often, either. When asked what religious views her family held, Ruth says, *"Just Protestant. My grandfather was a Spiritualist—the Steeles were Spiritualists—but my father was not. I'm not so much, but my mother was religious and my sister Sandra is.*

"We went to the Congregational Church down here in Pescadero, but we weren't regular, you know, it was hard coming in to town. They had church release time [from school] every Tuesday, so that's when I went to church when I was growing up."

As teenagers the Steele girls would go to Santa Cruz more often. *"We used to take piano. [Cousin] Jan [Elliott] and I, and Sandra, used to take piano lessons down at Santa Cruz. One of the mothers, or sometimes both of them, would go too. I took guitar*

Clifford Moore proposed to Ruth Steele while he was serving "Uncle Sam" in Germany. Their marriage, on February 18, 1956, joined their families again 75 years after Charlie Steele married Ida Jane Moore. This year (2006) they celebrated their 50th wedding anniversary.

lessons and Sandra took steel guitar lessons. Then Jan started taking piano and I took piano. Every Saturday we'd go to Santa Cruz."

Ruth's life growing up at the Chalk Ridge farm changed dramatically when she was in high school. Her grandmother, Lou, whom she loved dearly, died in 1954. Within two years, Ruth would embark on an entirely different phase of her own life's journey.

THE CIRCLE IS COMPLETE

The reason Ruth moved to Pescadero and has stayed here is because she married Clifford Moore. The first time she met Clifford, it was on her father's ranch. Clifford's father, Alec Moore, brought his boy with him one time when he came down to buy some grapevines from the Steeles. Ruth was only 2 at the time and Clifford, age 7, was significantly older. Her mother says that Ruth must have liked Clifford right away because she did something little girls do when they like someone by giving him something that belonged to her. In Ruth's case it was a set of dishes, but Clifford, apparently at a loss as to what to do with them,

immediately pitched them over a bank. Ruth's mother was furious and retrieved the dishes as soon as the Moores left.

Ruth and Clifford didn't meet again until they were both in high school in Pescadero; she was a freshman, he was a senior. Ruth can't remember their first date—maybe it was a school dance—but she says they started "seeing each other" when she was 13. Every once in a while they would break up and date other people, but the spark between them never really went out. Maybe it was that exciting motorcycle Clifford rode around on.

Clifford graduated from school three years ahead of Ruth in 1952, and worked in the oil industry locally for a year or so. In 1953 he went away to serve in the Army. It was a classic case of absence making the heart grow fonder, for that was when Ruth started thinking he might be "the one." Clifford, stationed in Germany, wrote casual notes to Ruth and she, still in high school, answered him back. They kept up their correspondence for two years. When she was "Sweet 16" Ruth received a letter from Clifford that finally went beyond casu-

al—it was a proposal of marriage.

Ruth graduated in 1955; Clifford returned from Europe. Ruth liked Clifford because he was honest, and ambitious. Most importantly, Ruth knew he was a good person and she felt safe with him. They were married on February 18, 1956 at the Pescadero Community Church in the first wedding ceremony new minister Orrill Fluharty ever performed. The bride was just a couple months' shy of turning 18. Ruth says she was too young, but that's what women did in the '50s—they didn't have careers, they got married—but it worked out.

"I was a young child-bride when I came here [to Pescadero] and I didn't know too much about cooking. Fannie Steele was a cousin of mine—she lived next door—and she helped me a lot. Fannie taught me how to cook venison and abalone; she was the one who helped me with my first turkey."

Clifford worked long days driving truck for the Tesi Drayage Company for 12 years; then with the San Mateo road department until he retired in 1993. Ruth looked after the ranch and raised three kids: Marilyn, James, and Barbara.

"I enjoyed my children. I was lucky, I was a stay-at-home mom. I didn't work. Clifford held down two-and-a-half jobs to keep us afloat, as he thought it was important that I stay home. The kids all turned out to be great kids. I think it was worth it. I had Marilyn in '58, Jimmy in '60, and then Barbara came along in '63. They were spaced nicely. I enjoyed the kids even when they were in high school, we had a lot of fun."

When she had a spare moment, Ruth helped out around town in school events, fundraisers, and public health services. She was known among her friends as the perfect person to kick up her heels for local stage productions, too! Every year the Moores packed the kids and whatever dog they had at the time and took their vacations exploring the country much in the same spirit of adventure as their ancestors did, albeit more comfortably in their house trailer. To this day, it's one of their favorite things to do.

Left: *A buggy crosses the bridge at Bean Hollow. 1890s-1900s.*
Below: *Muriel Steele Olund (left) and Catherine Baumgarten Steele (Mrs. Will Steele) in the yard at Green Oaks. 1920s.*

Sources

All photographs are from the Ruth Louise Steele Collection archived in the Pescadero Historical Society inventory unless otherwise noted.

Conant, Edward — *Memories of Gazos Creek and Pigeon Point, 1916-1918.* Glenhaven Press; Modesto, CA.

Koch, Margaret — *Santa Cruz County Parade of the Past.* Valley Publishers; Fresno, CA, 1973.

Koch, Margaret — *His Memories Go Back Almost a Century,* [from "Santa Cruz County Parade of the Past."] loaned by Ruth Moore as a separate piece.

Latta, Frank F. and Jean M. — *"Gazos Ranch."* Manuscript 68-152 from the San Mateo County History Museum Archives.

74-17 *Letters* — San Mateo County History Museum Archives: Box containing correspondence between J.C. Williamson of the Pescadero Creamery and several agents in San Francisco regarding shipments of cheese and butter, around 1900.

Lyon, Mary Louise — *"A Portion of the History of the Patrons of Husbandry in San Mateo County 1860 to 1900."* Student monograph 1800 SM from the San Mateo County History Museum Archives.

Mowry, Harvey — *Echoes from Gazos Creek Country; San Mateo County's South Coastal Region.* Edited by Mary E. Guzman. Printed and published by Mother Lode Printing; Jackson, CA.

Starr, Kevin — *Americans and the California Dream 1850 – 1915.* New York; Oxford University Press; 1973.

Steele, Catherine Baumgarten and Wilfred H. Steele [compiled by] — *The Steeles of Point Año Nuevo, A Family Genealogy and History from 1591 – 2000;* updated version, 2000.

Steele, George H. — *"The Steele Family of Pescadero."* Student Monograph 963 from the San Mateo County History Museum Archives. January 1948.

Steele, Ruth Louise — "Notes from videotape made in Rita's Hair Salon," May 20, 2003 and *"Interview with Ruth Louise Steele Moore"* in her home, Pescadero, April 11, 2005. Pescadero Historical Society.

Pescadero in the early 1890s – 1900.

About the author

Tess Black is a first-generation California native. Born in Culver City, she was raised in Long Beach but summered every year with her mother's relatives on a Virginia farm that has been in her family for five generations. These childhood experiences fostered a passion for uncovering hidden stories from the past. Later she graduated with a degree in cultural anthropology from the University of California at Berkeley, but, sidetracked by her interests in writing, art, and photography, she ended up in a graphic arts career working for publishing houses first in the Bay Area and then in Honolulu, Hawaii. She lived in the Islands for 21 years before returning to California six years ago.

She now lives with her husband in the redwood forests of Loma Mar—formerly Harrison Canyon—six miles up the creek road from Pescadero town and works as a freelance writer, editor, and publications designer. This is her first book.

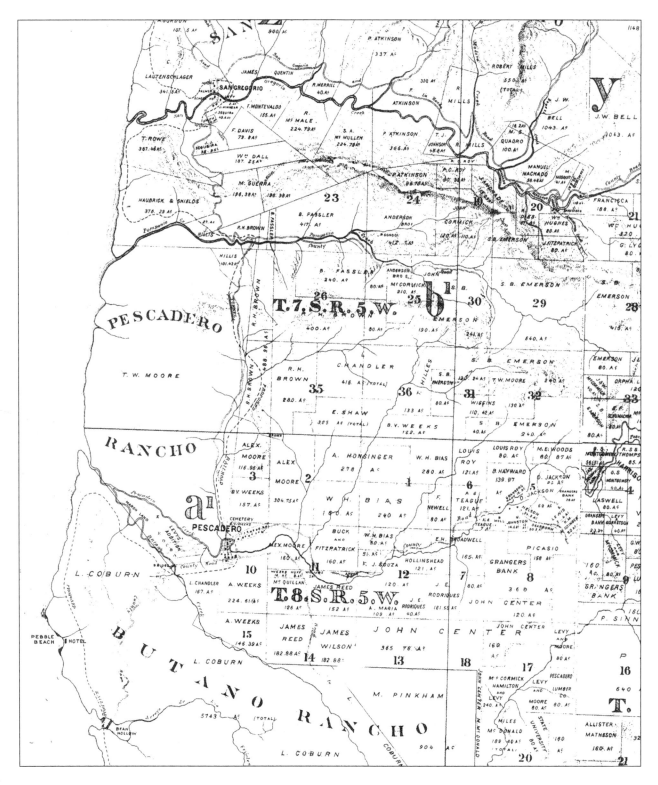

The lands of Rancho Pescadero, 1894
Map of San Mateo County; San Mateo County Historical Museum